"Improvement is the goal"

Approachable

"Leadership, according to Joe Franklin, comes from 'common sense and accumulated wisdom.' Trouble is common sense doesn't turn out to be all that common, and wisdom can be elusively hard to accumulate. A handy solution to that dilemma is this fascinating book. No mechanical how-to manual, it's brimming with easily relatable, personal experiences and thoughtful observations. In the process, it provides any number of keen insights into what leadership is really all about. There's something valuable here for *everyone*."

—PETER M. DAWKINS
Brigadier General, U.S. Army (Retired)
Vice Chairman, Citigroup Global Wealth Management

"For sure in the Armed Forces, physical courage and strength are important, but what struck me most of all about General Joe's excellent book is the extent to which the virtues of leadership are also the virtues of any good, well-rounded human being: approachability, responsibility, and integrity; compassion, vision, and faith. What West Point ultimately does is allow and encourage all cadets to be the best that they can be—with the knowledge that being the best means living by the highest standards. Joe also makes the point that each of us—to a greater or lesser extent—has the ability within us to do that."

—WILLIAM H. ROEDY
Vice Chairman, MTV Networks, and
President, MTV Networks International

BUILDING LEADERS WEST POINT WAY

THE

★ ★ ★

TEN PRINCIPLES FROM THE NATION'S MOST POWERFUL LEADERSHIP LAB

MAJOR GENERAL JOSEPH P. FRANKLIN
U.S. ARMY (RETIRED)
with Joe Layden

THOMAS NELSON
Since 1798

NASHVILLE   DALLAS   MEXICO CITY   RIO DE JANEIRO   BEIJING

Published in Nashville, Tennessee. Thomas Nelson is a trademark of Thomas Nelson, Inc.

Thomas Nelson, Inc. titles may be purchased in bulk for educational, business, fund-raising, or sales promotional use. For information, please e-mail SpecialMarkets@ThomasNelson.com.

Library of Congress Cataloging-in-Publication Data

Franklin, Joseph P.
    Building leaders the West Point way : ten principles from the nation's most powerful leadership lab / Joseph P. Franklin with Joe Layden.
        p. cm.
    Includes bibliographical references and index.
    ISBN-13: 978-0-7852-2164-7 (hardcover)
    ISBN-10: 0-7852-2164-6 (hardcover)
    1. Leadership. I. Layden, Joe. II. Title.
    HM1261.F73 2007
    303.3'4—dc22

                                                            2006038452

Printed in the United States of America

07 08 09 10 QWM 5 4 3 2 1

★ ★ ★

Leading soldiers in America's army was a privilege I could not have imagined as a youth. To then become a senior executive in our nation's business circles gave added dimension to a life already full. All of these experiences, opportunities, and achievements, the hard work done and warm relationships shared, would have never come to pass without the support of seniors, peers, and subordinates who served with me throughout the years. They are the soldiers, sailors, airmen, and marines whose names are too many to list here, but they are represented today by the men and women who risk their lives every hour of every day to defend our freedom.

I am one of those upon whom fortune smiled. My wife, Connie, and I have been blessed with good health, and wonderful children and grandchildren to love and cherish. Our life together has been greatly enriched by lifelong friends from many corners of the earth. Those are, truly, the foundation stones of a life that allowed me to be the best I could be.

For all these good fortunes, I offer thanks every day to the men and women who serve our country, and to my family, who made it possible for me to serve them.

—JPF

CONTENTS

FOREWORD

I first met Joe Franklin in 1953, when we were cadets at West Point. Although not physically imposing, he was sufficiently gifted to make his mark at the Academy. Not only did he win varsity letters in football and golf, a unique achievement in any man's book, he also won the heavyweight wrestling championship of the Cadet Corps.

Now with all those athletic awards, one might conclude that here was just another typical jock who could compete in sports but not much else. But I also remember Joe's graduation—one year before mine—when he walked across the dais, near the top of his class academically, to receive his diploma and commission from President Dwight D. Eisenhower. To anyone who was paying attention, this was a young officer with the potential to reach for the stars.

As happens so often in army careers, Joe and I subsequently found ourselves together in teaching assignments at the Military Academy, battalion commands in Vietnam, and staff positions in the Pentagon. It was not hard to keep track of Joe during those years. His thoughtful style of leadership and interpersonal skills soon put him ahead of his peers as our careers progressed from company grade duties to general officer responsibilities. At each level, his ability to look ahead, adapt to change, and lead others to get the job done earned him the opportunity to reach higher. When we spoke of Joe Franklin in those days, it was with respect for his integrity and quiet determination and with affection for his approachability and compassion. His genuine care for others, subordinates and peers alike, set him apart as one of the army's top leaders in our day.

So now he has shared his thoughts about those years of leadership in this book: *Building Leaders the West Point Way: Ten Principles from the Nation's Most Powerful Leadership Lab.* These are important lessons for nascent leaders, whether they be in the ranks of the military or the offices of corporate America. I especially like the way this book makes the point that leadership is caught, more than it is taught.

What impresses me most, and what I think makes this such a useful book, is how it applies directly to the individual reader. It is a book that describes real-life lessons from the author's personal experience that anyone can adapt to his own personality and skill set. As Joe says, you don't have to be seven feet tall or eat nails for breakfast. You can take each of these principles, adjust it to your own situation, and you will find that it really works for you. Taken together, these ten principles form the building blocks for a successful career in leadership in every walk of life—be it the military, profit or nonprofit corporations, teaching, or coaching—you name it.

I think it is emblematic of Joe's thoughtful approach to leadership that he urges readers, at some point in their own careers, to share their thoughts on this subject just as he has done. None of us has a monopoly on wisdom and quoting from Joe's book: "I can't really define leadership, but I know it when I see it."

—GENERAL H. NORMAN SCHWARZKOPF

INTRODUCTION

I really can't define leadership, but I know it when I see it.
—ANONYMOUS

Want to hear something funny? I thought about attending one of the great Ivy League schools but decided to try for West Point instead. When I accepted an appointment to the United States Military Academy in 1951, however, I had no idea that military service was part of the deal. Honest to goodness. Somehow or other, the fact that I was obligated to enter the United States Army upon graduation had escaped me. That was surely more of an oversight on my part—I was kind of a naive kid from the mountains of western Maryland—than any lack of disclosure on the part of the Academy. But I can tell you this: it wouldn't happen today. Cadets in the twenty-first century, men and women alike, arrive at West Point with eyes wide open, eager to embrace the ideals espoused and taught by the Academy, to serve their country and to follow in the footsteps of the great leaders who have come before them. In so many ways, they are the best and the brightest, and I am not only proud to be considered among them but also fortunate to have had the opportunity to teach them and to learn from them.

Indeed, almost everything that I am as an adult—everything I have accomplished and learned, successes earned and disappointments endured—can be traced back to my days at West Point. That's one of my primary motivations for writing this book. *Building Leaders the West Point Way: Ten Principles from the Nation's*

Most Powerful Leadership Lab is, at least in part, an attempt to share my life experiences with others, especially young people, so that I can try to help them achieve their goals. I believe in the West Point methodology, vision, and philosophy. They worked for me, and they have worked for countless others. But you don't have to graduate from the U.S. Military Academy to embrace its ideals, or to benefit from the wisdom that is taught there.

You don't have to be beautiful or handsome or brilliant to be a good leader, but you do need dedication to your mission and a strong belief in what you are doing.

I am, by nature, a fairly humble and self-effacing individual. But this is a personal book, and as such it will draw less on the exploits of West Point's famous graduates such as Douglas MacArthur, Dwight Eisenhower, and Omar Bradley, than on my own firsthand experiences. I may refer to some of these people from time to time, in passing, but the intent is not to say, "Here is a great example of how to be a leader . . . just be like MacArthur." That's a bit daunting for anyone. And besides, there is already no shortage of material to be found on the lives of America's greatest military leaders. This is a different type of book, and its message applies to everyone. You don't have to be six foot six to be a good leader. You don't have to be an all-American football player, and you don't have to be a brilliant Rhodes Scholar. While it certainly is an advantage in any walk of life to be intelligent, articulate, and physically endowed, the capabilities required of a strong leader are not terribly unique. In fact, quite the opposite is true.

Competent, even inspiring, leadership is within the grasp of nearly everyone. It doesn't matter whether you can play the piano or speak five different languages; it doesn't matter if you can run a five-minute mile. You don't have to be beautiful or handsome or brilliant to be a good leader, but you do need dedication to your mission and a strong belief in what you are doing. Becoming a leader is as much about marshalling the abilities you have as anything else. Talent is overrated. The roadside is littered with people who didn't know what to do with their talent, or who didn't care enough to make the most of their gifts. Even at seventy-three years of age, I still, each night before I go to sleep, evaluate the day that has passed and what I have done with it. I ask myself a simple question: *What do I need to work on?*

So far, the answer has never been . . . *Nothing.* And I suspect it never will be.

The modern U.S. Army is, in almost every way, the most egalitarian element of our entire society. It's a fair workplace with a simple ethic: if you're good at your job, you move up, without question—regardless of ethnicity, religious preference, or socioeconomic background. How far you go depends on a number of factors, only one of which is talent. Ambition plays a certain role, as does timing, and of course, there's always an element of chance.

Surprisingly enough, while the real world is a very political place, the army is not. Oh sure, there is the equivalent of water-cooler conversation—"Hey, the CO likes Captain Jones. How much would you like to bet he gets the next company command?" More often than not, though, the reason for job selection and moving up the ladder is outstanding performance.

One of the reasons why the army is such a great preparation for life is that senior officers are always on the lookout for talented younger folks. But just like anywhere you go in life, the learning curve varies. Some young men and women in the military will shoot ahead for a while and then get reeled back in. But it tends to even out over the long run. And no matter how the promotion happens, there is no substitute for hard work and dedication. They always pay off.

There is an obvious mission at West Point, and that is to train officers for the army, and for service to their country—for life. But who knows at age seventeen, eighteen, or nineteen whether they really want to serve a full career in the army? I had no idea. Today I suspect the great majority of young cadets arriving at West Point probably feel more committed to the notion of a military career than I did. That's certainly reassuring—they probably *should* feel that way if they're accepting an appointment to the Academy. They should have some inkling that the lifestyle suits them. But the truth is, they don't really know. They can't know. Not at that age. Once they enroll at the Academy, if we're doing our jobs as army leaders, things will begin to fall into place. We'll teach them to be the best officers and leaders they can be. And when they graduate, they will be guaranteed a good-paying, very responsible job that will be like no other they could find anywhere else in the world.

Where else will you turn from carefree college days and find yourself with fifty or more men and women standing before you, waiting for you to tell them what to do? That's real responsibility. And when cadets graduate we can tell them in all candor and sincerity: When you put on those insignia of rank, you'll be good at your job, and if you're good at it, you'll probably like it. And if you like it, you'll probably stay in and move up in the army.

If they decide instead to look outside the army, history tells us they'll have no trouble landing a corporate job, and they'll be good at that too. Eventually, that will lead a great majority of them back to service of some kind that helps our nation in many different ways.

There is a proven formula at West Point, a method for cultivating leaders. But please do not think that the formula has never been adjusted or tweaked. Tradition is a wonderful thing, but complacency and stagnation are not. There was a period of time when change was neither embraced nor accepted by the Academy, but that is not the case today, and I would wager that it never will be again. In any organization, change is inevitable . . . and positive. With training and experience, we come to recognize in advance when change is necessary, rather than having it foisted upon us in a crisis situation.

One of the ways this is encouraged at West Point, and in the military in general, is through intense interaction between teachers and students, leaders and subordinates. Younger cadets at West Point look to the people who are in charge—officers and older cadets— and glean little bits of information and examine them over time, holding on to things they find work for them and casting aside things that do not. It may seem like a subtle difference, but it's really crucial to the notion of producing effective leaders—and West Point, not coincidentally, has always turned out far more than its proportional share, and always will in this man's view.

In any organization, change is inevitable . . . and positive. With training and experience, we come to recognize in advance when change is necessary, rather than having it foisted upon us in a crisis situation.

U.S. Military Academy graduates are found in every walk of life: military, education, business, medicine, law, government. Name a field, and chances are that Academy graduates can be found at its highest levels of achievement. I don't think that's an accident. True, the cadets at West Point are almost universally motivated and focused young men and women—they have a natural desire to succeed and lead, and to do the right thing. But remember, leadership must be caught as well as taught. Setting the right example is absolutely essential to leadership. You can't teach people how to be leaders if they can't catch the idea from you, and you have to be aware of where they're coming from so you can guide them to where they need to go. That's a cornerstone of the West Point experience: cadets interact on a daily basis with officers who have gone through the experiences that they themselves will encounter when they are commissioned, with life-and-death responsibility for their subordinates.

The benefit of this atmosphere is almost immeasurable, for nobody is born with the innate capabilities of Douglas MacArthur, but everyone—and I mean everyone—has qualities and capabilities that portend success. Leaders have to be molded from these qualities, making the most of their inborn characteristics. We all come from different backgrounds with different strengths and weaknesses. History tells us that some of us will wind up succeeding and leading while others will fall short of their potential.

West Point forced me to discipline myself early in life. As an adolescent I had enough academic, athletic, and social talent that I probably could have coasted a long way, and people would have been generally supportive. This is all hindsight, of course, but I know now that what I learned at the Academy—self-discipline and respect for others at the head of the list—was the key to the success I've enjoyed in my life. I am fortunate to have found success in the military and in the private sector, as well as in my personal life. I've been blessed in countless ways.

Would so much good fortune have been bestowed upon me had I gone to another fine institution of higher learning, as I nearly did? I don't know. I do believe that somehow my little moral compass—God silently pointing in the right direction—told me, "This is the right thing for you to do, sonny." In the classic struggle between right and wrong, right would have triumphed; I feel certain of that.

But, with apologies to Robert Frost, I took the road less traveled, and that has made all the difference. I can't imagine that anything other than a West Point education, coupled with the military career that followed, would have given me the kind of opportunities to contribute to society that I was fortunate enough to experience. From the Academy—where I was not only a cadet but an instructor, football coach, and eventually commandant of cadets—to field assignments in such disparate lands as Vietnam and Greenland and to military and diplomatic positions in the Pentagon and Spain, I've been to so many places where I woke each day knowing in my heart that the work I was doing really mattered and that I was helping other people.

Had I had spent my formative (i.e., college) years in some other environment, I don't believe I would have accomplished nearly as much. Just as it has to so many others, West Point gave me the tools and the guidance to live a full and rich life, a life of leadership and service. Simply put, West Point gave me the education, training, and inspiration that set me on a straight course, and that has made all the difference.

Allow me to add this footnote: the education and training given today at the U.S. Military Academy are far more advanced than anything we experienced back in the post–World War II or Korean War era. In fact, you can hardly make a comparison between the training I received and the training that all cadets go through today. Cadets who graduate today are ready to go to war, and they have to be. They are our first and best line of defense; if they can't do it, no one can.

If you're reading these words, you either see yourself as a leader or want to be a leader, and I hope that you can use this book as a dialogue rather than a lecture. The principles of leadership you'll find in each chapter can be internalized and polished to your own level of expertise and ambition. Regardless of your goals—whether you hope to be a great army officer, a corporate executive, or an inspirational teacher or coach—I believe you'll find something of value on these pages. This book isn't a self-help program; rather, it's a philosophical approach to becoming an effective leader.

Cadets who graduate today are ready to go to war, and they have to be.

Each of the chapters that follow is devoted to a specific principle of leadership. More accurately, it might be fair to say that each chapter describes in detail a characteristic that I believe is essential to good leadership. And you'll find that these principles are not independent of each other; they are bound together in a self-reinforcing mosaic that makes good leaders. This is what I found in my fifty-plus years as an army officer, a CEO, a teacher, and a coach. It worked for me, and it'll work for you too.

LOOKING BACK

You can't get there from here; you've got to go someplace else first.

—NEW ENGLAND HUMOR,
FROM A STORY TOLD IN MAINE

In America, it isn't where you start in life that counts. Well, that's not entirely true, of course—some have it easier than others. But with the proper combination of ambition, talent, and support, almost anyone can find happiness and success, regardless of his roots.

Mine were certainly humble enough. I grew up in Cumberland—a small Appalachian town in western Maryland—without much exposure to the outside world, and much of my growing-up time was spent in the wilds of far-western Maryland at Deep Creek Lake in Garrett County, the original county in the Appalachian Regional Program. Considering that I was born at the height of the Great Depression, I was quite fortunate. My mother, my stepfather, and my grandparents took good care of my twin sister and me, and I never wanted for much of anything.

Educational opportunities, however, were limited in that region, so in sixth grade, I was sent to the McDonogh School, just to the northwest of Baltimore, where we students lived and worked on the grounds and the farm each day before classes. Funded by the estate of a philanthropist named John McDonogh shortly after the Civil War, the McDonogh School was originally designed as an educational setting for foundlings—street urchins who were, as often as not, the progeny of sailors stationed in the port city of Baltimore. By the time I arrived, McDonogh had evolved into something more refined, a traditional private school with a military bent. Eventually, I not only graduated from McDonogh but became a trustee as well, and the school continues to hold a place in my heart. It was, you see, the beginning of my experiences in self-discipline and leadership.

How and why I ended up at the United States Military Academy were not atypical for my generation. It's not that I had a burning desire to go there, and as I said, I didn't even realize I had to join the army when I enrolled (although, like most kids who grew up during World War II, I felt a certain romanticism about the notion of being a soldier). In eleventh grade, however, a thoughtful teacher suggested that the Academy might be a good fit for me.

Contributing to my decision was a weekend trip to Princeton University, where, as a football recruit, I was shown a reasonably good time. I can still recall, however, being in the men's room on Sunday morning and hearing the sounds of other students paying the price for the previous night's debauchery. And I remember thinking to myself, *I don't think this is right for me!* The U.S. Military Academy, with its promise of seriousness and discipline, combined with academic rigor, was the challenge that ultimately appealed to me. Somehow, I knew it was going to be the right place for me.

So I took the entrance exams and received an appointment, and off I went. It seemed a fairly natural and comfortable thing, going from McDonogh to West Point, even if I hadn't given it a great deal of thought. It's important to note that the generation from which I sprang—the Depression babies who grew up during World War II—was not particularly well oriented toward making plans for the future. Our plans were basically, *Okay, I've got that done; what should*

I do next? It was just not in our genes back then to make long-range plans and lay things out, step by step.

I sometimes tease youngsters at the Academy today because I'll hear them say, with a hint of panic in their voices, "Sir, I've got to take this course, then the follow-up courses, get past these exams, get this done . . . ," and so forth. I'll look at them seriously, give them a little smile, and say, "And if you don't, is that going to be the end of the world? Will your life be over?" The answer, rather obviously, is always no. I find that young folks always appreciate a bit of perspective, even the ones who have the goods to make it to West Point. It wouldn't surprise me that some of them imagine themselves moving up in the world, daydreaming of becoming a general officer, or president of the United States, or the chief executive officer of a Fortune 500 company. But life is a long, exciting ride, and no one can ever say for sure where the road will eventually go and how it will end.

Athletics were important to me at West Point, and I believe that some form of physical capability is important for a leader because it projects a competitive nature that any follower can see and understand. You don't have to demonstrate it or show it off, but for some reason that I've never quite been able to explain, I felt I had to make a mark in sports. I swam and wrestled and played golf, winning awards in all three sports, and I managed to earn a varsity letter in football. A "Major A" in football was no small achievement back then since Army routinely fielded one of the NCAA's most competitive teams (in an era when everyone had to play both offense and defense). But the interesting thing is that when I finally received my varsity letter after years of striving, it didn't seem like such a big event after all. I got my letter, held it in my hand, and thought, *What's next?*

I experienced a similar feeling a few years later when I received my two master's degrees from MIT (one in civil engineering and one in nuclear engineering). The hardest academic work of my life was rewarded not with an elaborate ceremony but with a quiet walk across campus to the registrar's office, where a busy young woman handed me a pair of diplomas and offered a perfunctory congratulations. Then she went back to work . . . and so did I. Maybe there's a life lesson there: It's a good and important thing to have goals in life—goals I would classify as short-term because they are achievable and seeable—as the result of the work you are responsible for and doing right now. But once you've accomplished those goals, you don't sit around and think about how great you are for getting to the finish line. You thank everyone who helped you get there, and you move on. Immediately.

Upon graduation I did all the usual macho stuff that West Point grads like to do: Ranger School, parachute school, combat engineer duty in postwar Germany, things like that. I had no real plan, just a desire to learn and to be challenged, and a faith that my hard work would be rewarded. (I also married the lady who came to all my birthday parties since we were two years old, went to kindergarten with me, and with another nod to Robert Frost, has made all the difference.)

Even with the background of McDonogh and West Point, I can't say that I had any clear idea what to do when I was handed my first platoon to lead. For grads today, that's definitely no longer the case. A great deal of the basics of leadership at the platoon level is learned at the Academy from the interaction between cadets and their noncommissioned officers. In every platoon in the army, there are several noncommissioned officers and one officer. Their roles are different, and a cadet needs to understand those differences before assuming command. Simply put, the noncommissioned officers "look in" while the commissioned officer "looks out."

I was fortunate to learn that lesson early in my army life, and I put it to good use during my time as commandant of cadets at West

Point. To assist the company tactical officers (the "tacs") in teaching and training the cadets, I brought in noncommissioned officers (the "tac NCOs"). I could only get one tac NCO for every battalion then, but today there's a tac NCO in every cadet company, and I think you'll not find one cadet in the entire Corps who does not understand their role and appreciate their presence. It is the tac NCOs who can tell the cadets precisely what their noncommissioned officers will expect of them when they take on their first army leadership duties, life-and-death responsibilities in the real world.

★ ★ ★

You will someday find yourself leading young people in jobs they have never done before. How you guide and mentor these young men and women will create lasting impressions. You never know until after the event, sometimes long after the event, what influence you may have had.

An early lesson in leadership, then, is how to handle the people you're working with, and the most important of those are the subordinate leaders whose jobs you have to recognize: they are the eyes and ears of a leadership that looks in. You don't do their job. Your duty is to create an atmosphere in which they can succeed at their job. It's about delegating authority, encouraging innovation, helping and coaching, and taking responsibility. That's the leadership that's taught at West Point.

My first assignment was in Germany, and I had a wonderful time there. I was newly married and soon became a young father. As is true with any job, I had a series of bosses, and naturally I liked some better than others. One man stands out, and this makes an important point: You will someday find yourself leading young people in jobs they have never done before. How you guide and mentor these young men and women will create lasting impressions. You never know until after the event, sometimes long after the event, what influence you may have had, but being aware of the impact you can have on young leaders is a very important characteristic of outstanding leadership.

My very special company commander was Colonel Eduard Scharff, U.S. Army, now retired. He was a veteran of World War II and the Korean War (and would soon become a veteran of the war in Vietnam). I learned a great deal from him, and we remain good friends to this day, which isn't unusual with military friendships—often forged under adverse and even life-threatening circumstances, they tend to withstand the test of time.

Next came graduate school at MIT, teaching and coaching assignments at West Point, and then immensely challenging tours of duty in Greenland and Vietnam. My assignment in Greenland was unique: I commanded a group of enlisted specialists sent to the polar ice cap to shut down, disassemble, and bring back to the United States a nuclear power plant. Nothing like this had ever been done before, and it won't be done again. We proved these nuclear power plants could be assembled and disassembled, and thus made portable; but we also determined, after eighteen months of hard, expensive work, in temperatures that routinely plummeted to eighty degrees below zero, that it wasn't very practical. The radiation levels we encountered there were another part of the story, but I'll save that for later.

The year I spent as a battalion commander in Vietnam was crucial to my development as an officer and a leader, in part, because Vietnam was a battalion commander's war. I led an independent combat engineer battalion that was not assigned directly to a higher tactical command. I started out in the Mekong River delta, moved to the central highlands, and passed through Cambodia before returning to the U.S. Mine was an important and life-preserving job, and I knew it. As a battalion commander in a time of war, you are always aware of one inescapable reality: there are going to be casualties. Your job is to accomplish the mission while protecting your people so you can continue to carry out other missions. It was an intensely demanding period for me, not least because we were always at risk of coming under fire, and the battalion was spread out from Qhi Nhon on the coast to Pleiku near the Cambodian border.

The truth is that every West Point cadet is primarily there to prepare to lead others into battle. Thankfully, we are not at war most of the time; nevertheless, educating, training, and inspiring young men and women who are prepared to fight the nation's wars are the *raison d'etre* of our military academies. Look at our history— we've been at peace much longer than at war. But, historically, we don't always come to the battlefield prepared. The reasons for this are more political than military, and are far beyond the control of the men and women who fight, but it's true nonetheless. The good news today is that we are no longer captive of that old problem of preparing for the "last war." There are terrifically innovative, forward thinkers in the military today—it's just a matter of their voices being heard.

I spent a large chunk of the seventies at the Pentagon where I held a variety of positions, including executive assistant to the chairman of the Joint Chiefs of Staff. While not as viscerally exciting as Greenland or Vietnam, Pentagon duty proved to be an invaluable experience because I was recognized by a number of senior officers. And it wasn't because of my blue eyes and disarming smile but rather because of my ability to think creatively and to fit ideas into the things that were going on around me and, by doing so, to subtly influence decisions. Call it diplomacy. Call it leadership. Call it what you will. My years in the Pentagon were an integral part of my education. I advanced to the rank of colonel and in 1978, at the age of

forty-five, found my name on the list of officers who were to be promoted to brigadier general.

I had no idea what assignment would accompany that promotion, and I have to say I was really surprised when I got a call from
General Andrew Goodpaster, the then superintendent of the U.S.
Military Academy. He asked me to travel to the Academy to be
interviewed for the position of commandant of cadets. (A note of
explanation here: at West Point, the superintendent's role parallels
that of the president of a university, the commandant parallels the
role of the dean of students, and there is a dean of the academic
board who oversees the academic side of the Academy.) General
Goodpaster, who passed away not long ago, was one of our country's greatest military leaders and an icon of the army. In his office
were huge framed portraits of former superintendents, including
Douglas MacArthur and Robert E. Lee. Needless to say, during my
interview for the job, I felt like a little kid in short pants.

"I would like to know what would be in your mind if I selected
you to be the next commandant," General Goodpaster said.

I thanked him and blurted out the first thing that occurred
to me.

"General Goodpaster," I said, gesturing with my hands on
opposite sides of my chair, "my image of the commandant, and my
image of myself, are poles apart."

The commandant, you see, is traditionally viewed as a stern dis-
ciplinarian, an intimidating man whose primary role is to enforce
regulations and mete out punishment. I just couldn't picture myself
like that. But General Goodpaster must have seen something in me
that he wanted in the commandant, and he chose me for the job.

Being asked to serve as commandant of cadets was a singular
honor, and it was never in my nature to hesitate or ruminate when
I was told what my next duties would be. If that was what the army
and, in this case, General Goodpaster told me to do, then I was

their man. It goes without saying that this first assignment for a plebe general was truly one of the most rewarding of my career or, as a matter of fact, of anyone's career. It's one of life's greatest rewards to see so many of those young men and women—cadets when I was their commandant—now commanding battalions and brigades all around the world in the war against terrorists. It's extremely satisfying to get calls and e-mail messages from them, to hear of their successes and achievements, and to think that I helped them along the way.

One even invited me to the Pentagon to have lunch with him not so long ago. At the time, he was Brigadier General Bob Caslen, running the anti-terrorism desk in the Plans and Policy Directorate of the Joint Staff. He'd been an assistant football coach at the Academy when I was the commandant; I recruited him to be a tactical officer, and that changed his career. And by the time this book is published, he will be the new commandant of cadets at West Point. Time and again, those kinds of rewards come back to you when you've served as "the Comm," and when it happens, there's no feeling quite like it.

> It's one of life's greatest rewards to see so many of those young men and women—cadets when I was their commandant—now commanding battalions and brigades all around the world in the war against terrorists.

I held the post of commandant until 1982, when I took over as assistant division commander of the Twenty-fifth Infantry Division in Hawaii. That was my last tour with troops, and being in such a great, active infantry division, training with soldiers every day, was a wonderful capstone to my career. A year later I was promoted to major general and appointed chief of the Joint U.S. Military Group and senior U.S. defense representative in Spain. Why Spain? Well, Spain was a particularly important country right then, having just joined NATO, and it was a sensitive stage in the development of relationships at that moment. So the army's chief of staff called me one morning while I was feeling pretty smug about myself in my office in Hawaii and said, "I need someone who can sit down to have a heart-to-heart talk with Jesus Christ without starting a fist fight before you're done." Somehow, I knew exactly what he was telling me, and I think he meant it as a compliment. I also knew that it was a terrific opportunity to serve in a really unique environment and set of circumstances and that it would be a serious challenge to my diplomatic and leadership skills. By the time I retired from the army in 1987, I had worked closely with just about all of Spain's major political and military players as they were joining NATO—King Juan Carlos, a wonderful man; all the Spanish chiefs of staff; and many other senior military and diplomatic figures in the new Spanish democracy, one of whom eventually became ambassador to the United States.

My wife and I elected to stay in Spain after my retirement, in part, because I just couldn't see myself back in Washington, D.C., playing a lot of golf and consulting on the occasional defense project. We still felt young and energetic, and the kids were out of the house, so we decided to have a little fun and start our own Spanish company. My wife did protocol work setting up events for the Olympics, the World's Fair, the five hundredth anniversary of Columbus's historic voyage, and Spain's entry into the European Union and Common Market, all of which took place in 1992. I worked on private business mergers and acquisitions. Spain was a great place for business at the time because American firms could finally invest in Spanish companies and vice versa. I was the middleman on a number of those transactions. It was a real learning experience for me to play a part in this new environment of civilian business and interpersonal relationships among disparate groups and individuals. And speaking another language added a special flavor to the mix.

We returned to the United States in 1993, when I accepted a position as chairman of the board and chief executive officer of Frequency Electronics, a Long Island–based American Stock Exchange (now NASDAQ) company that builds critical time and frequency systems for the defense industry. The company recently had been hit with a whistle-blower lawsuit, and my job, as someone who wasn't even remotely connected to the allegations, was to bring some much-needed stability to the company. The fact that the lawsuit was specious was irrelevant; this was a time that earned the name *ill wind*, when accusations and indictments were flying and defense contractors were being taken to court and going to jail in droves.

I learned a real lesson in corporate leadership, which boils down to this simple piece of advice: you have to surround yourself with good people who know what they're doing and feel comfortable being totally honest with you.

At Frequency Electronics we had a tough time of it, and for me, it was an ill-defined and tension-filled way to break in as a CEO. Senior members of the company were under indictment, and I was to be the white knight who, hopefully, would get this all behind us and keep the company afloat. Sparing the details, after six long years of trying to explain that no one had done anything wrong, we were told, in effect: "It really doesn't matter if anyone is guilty or innocent; have the company plead guilty, pay cash, do it now, or else." And so that's how we settled the suit. It wasn't very glamorous or inspiring, but I was a better man for having gone through it. I suppose it's fair to say that I wound up a hero of sorts because the company survived and is now very prosperous in both government and commercial sectors, and I felt that I helped to resolve a much distorted situation while bringing some integrity and honor to a very seamy process.

I'm only the chairman of the board at Frequency now, but I learned a real lesson in corporate leadership, which boils down to this simple piece of advice: you have to surround yourself with good people who know what they're doing and feel comfortable being totally honest with you. If you don't have the technical knowledge to cover the complete spectrum of the job (and it is the very rare person who does), you have to be able to depend on others. But they also have to be straight arrows who will tell it like it is, and they have to be convinced that when they tell it, you will stand up for them.

In recent years I've devoted considerable time and energy to alumni affairs at the U.S. Military Academy. For me, that's a labor of love. After almost twelve years in the leadership of the board of trustees of the Academy's Association of Graduates, I recently stepped down from the vice chairman's job. This I did with no misgivings, actually, because one of the keys to good leadership is knowing when it's time for younger blood to take over. I say this here because there was, for a while, some pressure on me to become chairman, but I believed that it was just not the right thing for the Academy. I graduated in 1955, and the median graduation year of our alumni today is the class of 1984. There are forty thousand living graduates of the Academy today, and half of them are less than forty-five years of age. It's time to call on our younger graduates and give them the leadership roles. Quite frankly, just between us older folks, we have to admit that someday there's going to be a right time for each of us to ride off into the sunset. Good leadership includes the sense to do that when the right time comes. I'm looking forward to the trip.

Looking back on all those years, there was never a time, as far as I can tell, when life lessons were not being learned and relearned. Let me just cite three more of those lessons here before we look at the principles I want to talk about:

1. I don't imagine any of us would argue about the importance of recognizing and understanding the big picture, and growing into larger leadership responsibilities means the picture just gets bigger the further you go.

2. Whether you're a second lieutenant or a major general, you can't let your ego get in the way of your judgment. A lot of people have trouble with that. Experience has taught me that knowing when to reach out and say, "Hey, I need some help here," is an integral part of leadership.

3. Finally, no one is infallible. Even the greatest leaders must come to realize, one way or another, that their places in the universe have limits, and those limits will be reached with the inevitable passing of time.

My purpose in writing this book is not necessarily to help you avoid the pitfalls of our greatest leaders, or to produce the next General Douglas MacArthur. It's something simpler, maybe even nobler. I'd like to share with you some of the things I've learned in my years as a soldier, an officer, and a leader in the corporate and not-for-profit worlds, and how everything, for me, is filtered through the prism of the West Point experience.

Anyone who reads *Building Leaders the West Point Way* has to adapt the principles I've written down here to his own situation. I say this because it's important to recognize up front that we can't escape who we are, and we are all prisoners of our own experiences. The important thing is this: recognize that nothing is in the "too hard" box. Young people in particular, I think, are prone to hearing or reading the advice of someone who has succeeded in a particular field and thinking, *I can't do that. It's too hard.* But, in fact, there's nothing in life worth having that is ever too hard to achieve if you're willing to work for it. I'm living proof of that.

1

DUTY

To educate, train, and inspire the Corps of Cadets so that each graduate is a commissioned leader of character committed to the values of Duty, Honor, Country and prepared for a career of professional excellence and service to the Nation as an officer in the United States Army.
— United States Military Academy
Mission Statement

Duty: Robert E. Lee called it the most sublime word in the English language. In plain words, it means doing the right thing, when it should be done, without having to be told to do it. It connotes a sense of obligation, an understanding that you are part of something bigger. It is, of course, one of the first words embraced by a cadet at the U.S. Military Academy, and you'll hear it often today from the mouths of young soldiers in the Middle East, who, when asked why they are risking their lives so far from home, state simply and eloquently that they are just doing their duty.

A cornerstone of duty is discipline, and not the type of discipline that has anything to do with punishment or consequence. Discipline in a soldier refers to a willingness to do one's duty, carrying out orders faithfully, without question and in the best way possible as understood and seen in the mind and eyes of the soldier. In his address to the graduating class of 1875 at West Point, Major General John M. Schofield spoke the words that became known as Schofield's Definition of Discipline:

1

The discipline which makes the soldiers of a free country reliable in battle is not to be gained by harsh or tyrannical treatment. On the contrary, such treatment is far more likely to destroy than to make an army. It is possible to impart instruction and to give commands in such a manner and such a tone of voice to inspire in the soldier no feeling but an intense desire to obey, while the opposite manner and tone of voice cannot fail to excite strong resentment and a desire to disobey. The one mode or the other of dealing with subordinates springs from a corresponding spirit in the breast of the commander. He who feels the respect which is due to others cannot fail to inspire in them respect for himself, while he who feels, and hence manifests, disrespect toward others, especially his inferiors, cannot fail to inspire hatred against himself.

Keep this in mind: the first subordinate whom you must learn to discipline is the most unruly one you will ever encounter, and that is yourself. Until you are ready to embrace the concept of duty, and all that it implies, you can't hope to instill that same sense in others whom you lead or manage.

Understanding and internalizing the relationship between duty and discipline is a fundamental part of the education, training, and inspiration of leaders at West Point. In order to be able to do your duty, you have to be able to impose discipline because it often requires doing something you don't want to do. Whether on the battlefield or in the boardroom, a leader is someone who steps to the head of the line and does what is required—even if it is something that he or she may find difficult or distasteful. Moreover, leaders perform these tasks with a quiet resolve, as though they want the outcome to be successful; and they do not do so begrudgingly. Keep this in mind: the first subordinate whom you must learn to discipline is the most unruly one you will ever encounter, and that is yourself. Until you are ready to embrace the concept of duty, and all that it implies, you can't hope to instill that same sense in others whom you lead or manage. Being able to do that is the hallmark of successful leadership.

GOOD STEEL COMES FROM A HOT FIRE

Duty does not mean that one follows blindly. It means understanding what must be done, and doing it, regardless of how you might feel on a personal level. When I was commandant at West Point, I would hold meetings with the individual cadet companies on Saturday mornings. These were informal sessions designed to elicit candor and honesty from the cadets, to find out what was on their minds. We called these sessions *ethical doughnuts*. The discussions were meant to let the cadets know that their officers were willing, and even eager, to hear their opinions and concerns. As often as not, the conversation would turn to matters of history and tradition— the cadets were naturally inquisitive and wanted to know why they were asked to perform certain tasks that, to their minds, were dull, repetitive, or unnecessarily difficult or time-consuming. Sometimes I could give them a short, convincing answer, and sometimes the answer was a bit long-winded and complicated. But if I was stuck for an answer, I could always resort to an old standby: "Ladies and gentlemen, good steel comes from a hot fire."

We'd all have a good laugh at my non-answer, in part, because we understood the truth behind the aphorism. There are times when you do something simply because it's there to be done or because it just seems like the right thing to do—and almost always because you are obeying rules that say you have to do it.

Obedience is a word that can have a negative connotation, as if it is at odds with traits that are often deemed more enlightened or admirable. This is particularly true in American society, since we are such an adventurous and questioning people. I believe, however, that there is no central conflict between obedience, which is a fundamental component of duty, and inquisitiveness. I look at obedience as a guiding light: *I'm doing this because it's the right thing to do. Someone told me this and I believe it.* Now because I'm an American, and especially because I have a responsibility as a leader, I'm always questioning, always looking for a better way to accomplish what needs to be done. That should be a source of pride, not shame, and that's how it is viewed at the Academy. Sometimes a young leader says, "Oh, my gosh, I thought I was doing the right thing and it turned out all wrong." Well, interestingly enough, in the army we consider that to be a very useful and important growing experience. Granted, mistakes can be costly, whether in business or in the military. But a young army officer who is trying to do the right thing will almost always be recognized by his or her superiors, and good leaders will keep the young folks on track.

FIRST SUMMER: BEAST BARRACKS

Intense, up-close, and personal exposure to West Point leadership begins the first day a freshman ("plebe") arrives at the Academy's new cadet barracks, which bears the historic and whimsical title of "Beast Barracks." This first day is the start of a six-week summer training session. Plebe summer remains the most difficult and arduous period for new cadets and with good reason. It is a completely new experience—a fast-paced, high-pressured test of the new cadets' abilities to manage themselves in such a demanding environment.

Historically, it is the period that accounts for almost half of all the attrition that a class will suffer during their four years at the Academy. It is emotionally and physically exhausting, and it sets the tone for the entire West Point experience.

Call it baptism by fire, call it immersion therapy . . . call it what you will. The purpose is to carefully, thoroughly, and effectively indoctrinate the cadets and prepare each of them for four years that will culminate in their graduation and commissioning as an officer in the finest army the world has ever seen. New cadets emerge from the summer program with an understanding of what will be expected of them, along with a growing confidence that they can and will surmount any obstacles placed in their path.

I should point out that plebe summer has changed over time. While it stresses and tests even the most capable of cadets, it is, thankfully, far from the degrading experience that it was in the early part of the twentieth century. When General MacArthur became superintendent at West Point in 1919, he viewed the summer session as an opportunity to train young people properly, rather than just wear them down until they could no longer function. This latter practice, which had actually resulted in the death of one cadet several years before, had lasted many decades and become entrenched as tradition, giving it something of an untouchable status.

In retrospect it's not hard to understand how such practices came into being, but it's not easy to change them once ingrained. A lot of the behavior and training techniques prior to MacArthur's arrival had been sophomoric at best and brutal, even fatal, at worst. Suffice it to say that things changed dramatically under MacArthur. He implemented a system in which plebe summer represented a training opportunity not only for new cadets but also for the senior cadets who were in charge of the new cadets in Beast Barracks. Not surprisingly, MacArthur's reforms were resisted by many, cadets and officers alike, and he left the Academy with, in his view, the job unfinished.

Admittedly, ever since then, the treatment of plebes has been cyclical in nature, but MacArthur's reforms inexorably took on permanency, and today the training of new cadets reflects the maturity that is expected of officers-in-training.

Schofield's Definition of Discipline means a great deal to me and to all cadets, in part, because it's one of the first things you learn. And you absorb it at the same time that you are enduring basic training. I found this contradictory and exasperating as a plebe. I'd hear the words "not to be gained by harsh or tyrannical treatment" echoing in my mind, even as an older cadet screamed at me: "Pull your chin in, mister! Drop that bag! Turn around! Get out of my sight, you worthless . . . !"

★ ★ ★

While mission statements and philosophical musings are all well and good, it's crucial that we, as leaders, never cease to critically examine our actual behavior in the context of the principles we value as leaders.

I handled the abuse about as well as anyone, I guess, but I couldn't help wondering what was going on. On the one hand, I was required to commit to memory this great pronouncement by Schofield and his farsighted, thoughtful approach to discipline; on the other hand, my day was an endless barrage of insults and threatened punishment. There seemed to be a clear and obvious contradiction, and yet nobody bothered to express it! I wasn't the first to notice, of course, but I think it's important to remember that while mission statements and philosophical musings are all well and good, it's crucial that we, as leaders, never cease to critically examine our actual behavior in the context of the principles we value as leaders.

How does one reconcile Schofield's Definition of Discipline with the treatment of plebes in years gone by? Well, you can't. What you do is work to correct it. Now, something that has been in place for many years can't be changed overnight. Of the sixty major battles fought in the Civil War, fifty-five of them were commanded by West Pointers—on both sides. And the other five had a West Pointer commanding on one side or the other. That was a significant commendation for the training that military leaders received at the Academy during that time, so it's not surprising that there were few changes of any kind after the Civil War ended until General MacArthur arrived as superintendent, fresh from commanding the U.S. forces in Europe during World War I. That time between the Civil War and MacArthur's appointment is called the Frozen Period for a reason. The truth is, we were resting on our laurels. Warfare changed, people changed, the world changed, and culture changed. But the Academy didn't. That was a huge mistake. West Point produces leaders, and leaders must, at every turn, ask themselves the hardest of questions: *What are we doing . . . and why are we doing it?*

By the time I took over as commandant in 1979, West Point was in need of some change again, and I did my best to eliminate the sophomoric behavior that had crept in and passed itself off as training. Obviously there are and always will be traditionalists who, with every good intention, believe that degrading behavior—for example, placing cadets under extreme physical duress or withholding food as punishment—serves as some type of bonding exercise or a rite of passage. After all, they survived or believe they survived this sort of treatment, and clearly it made them better men, so why should things be any different? I strongly disagreed. "Ladies and gentlemen," I would announce, "we use food to train dogs and cats, not human beings." The focus should be to conduct professional, dignified training that instills positive skills and attitudes and to have that philosophy embraced as a permanent way of life.

> **West Point produces leaders, and leaders must, at every turn, ask themselves the hardest of questions:** *What are we doing . . . and why are we doing it?*

To the enormous credit of the people who run the modern United States Military Academy, that has happened, and I am quietly pleased to recall my part in keeping that transformation going and getting us to where we are today. We'll never go back. As with our liberty, however, eternal vigilance is essential to keep that transformation evolving so it will always reflect the up-to-date mores of our military training and culture. We have dispensed with any notion that new cadets are just dirt. They are, in fact, the best of the best of a new "greatest generation," and while we should test them and demand the most from them, we can and must treat them with dignity and respect—from day one. That is how you build leaders dedicated to the principles of this book, not through degradation and humiliation.

LEARNING RESPONSIBILITY

With arrival at West Point, and along with it the beginning of a lifetime sense of duty, comes responsibility. In a macro sense, responsibility means living up to the terms of the deal: a first-class education in exchange for service as an officer in the U.S. Army, which carries with it the serious burden of protecting our country and our citizens. On a much smaller, personal scale, responsibility means handling an assortment of tasks—from the mundane to the complex. A very simple job for new cadets is to be assigned the duties of the minute caller. When formations are due, one of the plebes in each section of barracks is required to stand out in the stairwell and shout updates to the company: "Sir, there are five minutes until assembly for parade! The uniform is as for class under raincoats . . . Sir, there are four minutes . . . three minutes . . ." The point is to assign them a responsibility. As often as not, plebes are out there in the hallway, reciting something that might not make a lot of sense to them, and thinking, *Why am I doing this?* Well, it's a responsibility. It's a duty.

From the very beginning, the West Point experience is one of being assigned responsibility, and not just personal responsibility—cleaning your rifle, storing gear in your locker correctly, making your bed—but responsibility that is woven into a much larger picture. There's a roster of tasks, and each cadet is assigned tasks that have an impact on the barracks and on other cadets. As training progresses, responsibilities grow. Older cadets are placed in positions of increased responsibility, which demand more of them as they, in turn, demand more of the cadets who are coming behind them. There is a whole litany of duties, from delivering mail to reporting class attendance to assuring that the dishes at each meal are properly served and divided. All kinds of small, menial tasks in the barracks, the mess hall, the classroom, and the athletic fields, the tasks that make everything function are handed out to the cadets. Could the barracks run in some fashion even if the cadets didn't do those things? Yes, of course . . . but by segregating out specific tasks and assigning them to cadets, they grow to internalize the serious nature of bearing responsibility and how that translates to duties performed. And that's beyond important. It's critical. In only four short years, these cadets are going to be leading the men and women who volunteer to wear the uniform of our country.

LEADING TO SERVE THE LARGER COMMUNITY

Academic training begins as Beast Barracks ends, and follows a similar path. There are countless tasks cadets are expected to do for themselves, and a myriad of others that support the day-to-day functions of life in the Corps of Cadets, doing their duties with academic schedules, physical education and athletic team assignments, and a host of other activities that are part of modern cadet life. By the time cadets finish plebe year, they're more than capable of meeting the minimum standards of duty; they're actually quite polished. Moreover, they understand that they are part of something much larger than themselves. Ambition is fine, and certainly there is no shortage of people who have become accomplished leaders primarily because they seek personal reward. But I believe that leadership is far more than just an award for doing well, and the philosophy of leadership training at West Point is not designed to promote that attitude.

The truth is, and I have come to know this from long experience, the best leaders are those who are committed to a sense of community, to creating an atmosphere of trust and goodwill. The best leaders are devoted to the people around them—family, friends, superiors, subordinates, and coworkers. And while I think most of us have an innate desire to help our fellow man, it is an emotion that can be honed and polished. West Point cadets finish their plebe year with the knowledge that they belong to a community and that the needs of the community come before the needs of the individual.

In many ways our society has become fractured. Young people are growing up without the experience of being part of a team and the sense of responsibility that goes with it.

Here's a simple example of how that works in the context of cadet life. Let's say one company of cadets is marching together in formation. If some of them are just slightly out of step, you'll see their heads bouncing up and down out of rhythm against all the other heads that appear to move in unison. It's very noticeable and un-military, and of course that's just not going to do the job. If some of the cadets are marching to the beat of a different drummer, so to speak, that needs to change—fast. If you are ever close enough to a cadet marching formation to hear their internal communications, you'll hear their voices correcting the out-of-step members of their company. That may seem like a small, frivolous example, but it's important because it reflects the value of working together for the good of the team. From these small incidents, cadets learn and recognize the value of teamwork very early in their experience: *I have a duty to do these things and do them right because if I don't, I hurt the team.*

In many ways our society has become fractured. Young people are growing up without the experience of being part of a team and the sense of responsibility that goes with it. Our spirit of individualism and tendency toward restlessness is at odds with the need to form and sustain viable, healthy communities. We live in far-flung, sprawling suburban communities that do not promote much in the way of personal contact or intimacy. In fact, we seem to go out of our way to isolate ourselves, listening to our own music, figuratively and literally, as we walk through the day. That's a shame—no, even more important, it's a societal weakness—because without a strong sense of community, we are prone to selfishness, and that threatens the foundation of any society. A good leader has to be very aware of this tendency and should always be on the lookout for ways in which to create and nurture a sense of community among subordinates. The best leaders will be intent on seeing that the people they lead feel that they are invested in something larger and more important than their own self-interests.

This is true not just in the military or political realms but in the business world as well. It's so important for all employees to feel that they are part of a team. The military has some obvious advantages in this regard because we gather people together countless times on a daily basis. If you visit West Point and watch a thousand or more cadets marching across the parade ground ("the Plain"), all dressed alike, all moving in this very measured, formal way, you get the distinct impression that each cadet has at some point internalized the message that he or she is part of a team. When an order is given to present arms, all cadets present arms in unison. When in formation, no one looks right or left unless commanded to do so. That is discipline. It's part of doing one's duty and doing it because of one's responsibility to the team.

Let's say that an order is given in the parade: "Eyes right!" This means that the cadets will turn their heads to the right as they pass in review and salute the reviewing officer. One particular cadet, as he raises his saber to salute, accidentally knocks off his hat. Does he stop the parade to go back and retrieve his hat? No . . . he keeps going and overcomes the natural instinct to correct the mistake because as powerful as that may be, it isn't always the right response.

I've seen more than a few hats fall to the ground during parades, and typically the response is to ignore it, just as I described. The cadet keeps right on moving because he knows that an attendant will pick it up after the entire parade has passed in review. More importantly, he knows that if he stops to retrieve the hat, the entire parade will lose its cadence, and the team will suffer. That may seem like a minor issue, but it illustrates a very fundamental element of leadership. It's about understanding one's duty, and fulfilling that duty even when something unexpected or unusual occurs and pulls us out of our comfort zone. In my experience, that's one of the great features of American military leadership: our officers and our noncommissioned officers have the ability and the wisdom and the training to discern the relative importance of a given event. And they know that if they fail, fall, or are injured, another will be there to help, to correct, or to carry on.

DUTY IS NOT ALWAYS BLACK AND WHITE

In keeping with the theme of community and teamwork, I think it's important to note that even duty is a principle with shades of gray. As with any organization, West Point cadets are expected to adhere to certain rules and regulations. Not surprisingly, however, during my three years as commandant at West Point, there were times and incidents when cadets misbehaved and broke the rules. Breaking the rules naturally provokes punitive measures of one sort or another. There are, after all, consequences to every action and reaction.

As commandant, my duty was to enforce the regulations, which included the discharge of any cadet who violated specific rules. That was my duty, though in each case that came before me I had to ask myself, *Is this really the right thing to do?* It would have been easy to just close my eyes and my mind and say, "Mister, you're out of here." But I had the latitude to take other factors into account. Duty, in every one of these cases, was not a cut-and-dried, mechanical thing. And for a leader, it seldom is.

I should note here that the final authority for discharging a cadet from the Academy rests with the superintendent. Thus, as commandant I had to explain and justify each disciplinary action I took when discharge was one of the options. The burden of laying out reasons for these decisions was not an easy one nor one that any of us took lightly, especially in the rigid regulatory environment we maintained as part of the image of West Point and what it meant to be a West Pointer. How could we exercise leniency when the rules were broken? And how could we be selective in doing so in some cases and not in others? This would be especially difficult and contentious in cases where violations spilled over into the realm of the Academy's Honor Code as I'll describe in the next chapter.

I don't mean to leave you with the impression that lenient treatment of serious violations is a common occurrence at West Point; rest assured, it is not. One of the wonderful things about the army and the Academy, however, is that even though the regulations are very carefully written, and strict guidelines are rigidly followed, we leaders have a very real amount of latitude to make decisions based on instinct and experience.

The success of the American army in war is directly traceable to the ability of its leadership to adapt to unforeseen events; and adaptability, as we will see in later chapters, is one of the guiding principles of good leadership.

Granted, by giving someone a second chance you are opening yourself up to criticism—of playing favorites and making decisions subjectively. Sometimes you're right, and sometimes you're wrong. But in my opinion and real-world experience, it would be a dereliction of duty to simply, coldly, and narrowly follow the regulations, without considering extenuating circumstances and making leadership decisions based on the broader interpretations that draw on one's highest sense of duty. The success of the American army in war is directly traceable to the ability of its leadership to adapt to unforeseen events; and adaptability, as we will see in later chapters, is one of the guiding principles of good leadership.

BEYOND THE CALL OF DUTY

It should come as no surprise that the higher you climb in the chain of command, the more likely you are to discover that there are many intricate layers within the definition of duty. For example, during my tour of command at Camp Century in Greenland, we lived in tunnels out on the polar ice cap, but at our base camp at the edge of the ice cap we lived on the surface in barracks built with insulated layers of plywood. We would pull back from working on the ice cap during the winter months, a long, brutal stretch of deep sub-zero weather with high winds and blinding snowstorms. When we were back at the base camp, we could work outside during good weather, but during the most severe weather, when our camp was being pummeled by storms categorized as Phase 3 (as opposed to Phase 1 or Phase 2), no one was permitted outdoors. Weather conditions were communicated by radio, and everyone understood and respected the parameters—in a Phase 3 storm, it was simply too dangerous to spend any length of time outside. Now, of course, if you had experience in the region, you knew where you could go and what you could safely accomplish, even in a Phase 3 storm. In general, though, the population of one hundred or so troops was required to remain inside those flimsy plywood barracks for the duration of a Phase 3 storm.

Well, we had one soldier who was assigned to take care of the utilities building—the nerve center for our electricity, water, sewer, and so forth—which was located several hundred yards from the barracks. His job—critical to our survival, and done entirely alone—was to remain in the utilities building when the storms hit and make sure things kept running properly. It was a hard and lonely job since these storms often raged for days on end.

During the course of one Phase 3 early in my command, as I was mentally cataloging the troops we had at the base camp, my mind lit on this particular youngster, riding out the storm in his lonely outpost. I had met him before, but I was fairly new at the camp, and given the nature of his duties, I wanted him to know that his effort was appreciated. The right thing to do, I decided, was to make my way down to the utilities building in the middle of the storm and let him know that we were thinking about him. So I did.

I knew that the troops would be surprised and impressed: "Wow! Did you hear that the captain went all the way down to the utilities building to check on Andy during that storm?" But in fact that wasn't the real reason why I did it. I did it because I knew instinctively that it was the right thing to do. And the young man, when I walked in to his little hooch, was shocked. He actually said, "Sir, I really appreciate and admire you coming down here just to make sure I'm okay." You can take it to the bank that all the soldiers at Camp Century knew the "old man" would look out for them.

Duty, Honor, Country is the motto of the U.S. Military Academy. *Money* doesn't appear in that motto. Not *profit* or *cash* or whatever. It's Duty, Honor, Country. The notion of accomplishing a particular mission or task, of course, folds into all three. Mission accomplishment focuses on *getting the job done.* But there is much more to duty. There is a context that goes beyond simply doing what you are supposed to do. It's doing the right thing, when it should be done, without having to be told to do it. And it's that last part that a leader has to learn and always keep in mind. Was it the right thing for me to walk outside into a Phase 3 storm? Only if I was reasonably certain that nothing bad was going to happen to me. If I'd gone out and realized that the storm was so fierce that there was a risk I wouldn't be able to get to the utilities building, I would have turned back. Why? Because my primary obligation was to take care of my troops. And that meant not taking unnecessary risks with my own life. No one had to tell me that. And I repeat: *unnecessary* risks.

> ★ ★ ★
>
> **There is a context that goes beyond simply doing what you are supposed to do. It's doing the right thing, when it should be done, without having to be told to do it. And it's that last part that a leader has to learn and always keep in mind.**

So what was my duty in that situation? Was it to uphold the rules and regulations that said I was not supposed to go outside in a Phase 3? I submit that a basic principle of duty is to be prepared to go beyond the rules when circumstances do not fit within the boundaries that the rules lay down. We've all known people in positions of leadership who feel so constrained by rules that they become ineffective. Fulfilling one's duty does not include a slavish adherence to limits. In fact, it means exactly the opposite. As Lee noted, *duty* is the most sublime of all words in our language. It is transcendent . . . and to a leader, it is the keystone that supports all others and on which success is built: doing the right thing, when it must be done, without having to be told to do it.

This is true in the business world as well. When I was invited to join the board of directors at Frequency Electronics after my initial work for them in Spain, I was greeted at my first board meeting with the news that, just the day before, the company had been raided by the FBI. The board members were understandably in shock; no one knew why Frequency had been targeted, and though they were certain that the company would be cleared of any wrongdoing, they would understand if I decided to resign from the board. I had to think about it for only a moment, just long enough to verbalize my sentiments.

"I've met you folks, and I know what you do," I said. "You've asked me to join the leadership of this company. That means you feel that I can make a contribution. Whether the company is running well or running poorly, that wouldn't enter into my calculation, so long as you feel there is something that I can offer. In other words, a duty I could perform." To close on a lighter note, I added, "And anyway, if you're going to be in a fight, it would probably be a good idea to have an army general on your side."

So I stayed on. I did not resign as a result of being confronted with an unknown. Now, I obviously knew that if this unknown turned out to be something that was really unsavory, I could disassociate myself from it. But further, this was a viable company that had developed certain advanced technologies that were critical to a number of key programs of the U.S. Government. No other company could replace these key technologies. Thus, that was also entering into my calculation: I believed that it was in the best interests of a great many people for this company to survive. And if they were in trouble, I would do my best to help them survive, regardless of the trouble. That was my duty: doing the right thing, when it should be done, without being told to do it.

THERE IS A TIME TO STEP DOWN

One final word here before we close this chapter on leadership and the principle of duty. There is a cycle to leadership, or it might be more accurate to say that the ultimate act of good leadership is to recognize that the role of leader does not last forever. It is, like all human acts, cyclical in nature. And thus a leader's duty also involves knowing when it's time to step aside. That's a difficult thing for almost all leaders, perhaps one of the most difficult things they ever have to do, particularly in the business world.

We have a built-in advantage in the military because we know we're only going to be assigned to a position for a certain length of time. When that time is up, off we go. We may move up, down, or

DUTY

sideways . . . but we do move. It's ingrained in the military persona
that there is no such thing as being commander or CEO for life. In
business, that's a much tougher issue to confront. Succession is
troubling for most organizations, even those that are exceedingly
well run.

Leaders in business will tell you that the most difficult challenge they face is the passing of the torch: the transition from one
chief officer to another. The reason for this is simple: it's hard to get
anyone to leave the corner office willingly. The life of the CEO is
often glamorous and seductive, not to mention financially rewarding. Is it any surprise that so many great leaders fail to recognize
when the time has come to step down? It's a sad fact that a lot of
successful businesses disappear after the founder leaves simply
because the one person who created the great enterprise finds it too
difficult to plan effectively for the future of the company. And so
all the sweat and blood that has made the company great is at
tremendous risk of going down the drain.

It need not be that way. A leader has an obligation, a duty, to
plan for the future, as we'll discuss in a later chapter. In fact, as I see
it from many years in retrospect, leaders have no more important
role than to nurture and protect those who work for them, who look
to them for guidance. And that means knowing how and when to
say good-bye.

2

HONOR

Ethics is our way of being human.
        —ALBERT SCHWEITZER

Regarded as the hallmark of a West Pointer, honor is a broad term that we can reduce to one simple phrase from the Cadet Prayer: "Choose the harder right instead of the easier wrong."

The words *ethics* and *integrity* also are used a lot in the post-Enron business world these days, usually in criticism of another's behavior: "If only he had some integrity, some sense of ethics, it never would have happened." Simple but true. I'm inclined to recall Albert Schweitzer's formulation: "Ethics is our way of being human." Great wisdom there. And human as it is, the most difficult thing a leader may ever encounter is an organizational tendency or culture that tolerates dishonorable behavior.

The Honor Code at the U.S. Military Academy makes toleration of an honor offense equivalent to committing an offense against the Code. Turning a blind eye is patently unacceptable. Sadly in our culture, adherence to an honor code is sometimes interpreted as the wrong thing to do—ratting out a friend, for example. But that's not what it's about. An honorable person does not condone dishonorable behavior, but confronts it to set things straight. That may be something as simple as talking to the offender: "Jack, you're my friend, and I know that what you did was wrong. Please, for the good of both of us, tell these folks what you did. They'll be compassionate if you admit you made a mistake. But if I have to tell them, you're putting a terrible burden on me, and I wish you wouldn't do that. It will be much harder on you if I'm the one who has to tell the story." That simple quote tells the whole story; that's the lesson that needs to be drilled home. At the age when cadets are learning this lesson, it is not easy for them to take it to heart, when personal relationships may be considered more important than a disembodied Code. At West Point, it's dealt with primarily in the performance of duties, military and academic, but eventually the real world will offer a test.

★ ★ ★

Whether a company operates within the parameters of a given lawful structure depends entirely upon the ethics of the leaders in place. Simply put, you can't legislate honorable behavior.

I've repeatedly noted in seminars and speeches that no matter how many laws are written, we will never stop corporate malfeasance. I'm sorry if that offends anyone, but that's reality. We can strive for nirvana, but we better be prepared for something less noble if we want to cope with the realities of everyday life. If stronger laws existed prior to Enron, Tyco, or WorldCom, criminal behavior still would have taken place because the people responsible for those scandals had lost sight of their ethical guideposts. Whatever laws might have been in place, they would have taken it upon themselves to figure out how to get around them.

Whether a company operates within the parameters of a given lawful structure depends entirely upon the ethics of the leaders in place. Simply put, you can't legislate honorable behavior. In the corporate world, there is a tendency to look at the numbers, promoting and rewarding the person who can produce the highest financial returns. That's all well and good and important for the shareholders who are depending on the leaders to generate good returns, but disaster lurks ahead if no one cares how the appointed leaders handle the inevitable ethical dilemmas. What if there's a problem and they're asked to cover it up? The right person to step up to leadership will always answer: "If that's the case, don't ask me to be in charge."

HONOR: CAUGHT AS WELL AS TAUGHT

Let's take a closer look at the way this principle is handled at West Point. Cadets are expected, at all times, to choose the harder right; they live by that creed. Now, that's a nice generalization, isn't it? But as Oliver Wendell Holmes famously pointed out, "No generalization is worth a damn—including this one!" So . . . what do you do when you think someone is doing something that violates the Honor Code? A cadet is bound by the Code. He or she "will not lie, cheat or steal, nor tolerate those who do." As noted above, the unique aspect of that statement, and the most difficult to internalize, is the nontoleration clause. It leaves no room for interpretation. The Honor Code defines honorable behavior. No question about it.

The undeniable truth, however, is that honor is like any other principle of behavior: it must be taught and absorbed in all its nuances before it can be applied fairly and effectively to its full, intended purpose. It's unrealistic to expect that everyone who arrives at West Point in that unformed state we call plebe will instantly comprehend and abide by every facet and nuance of the Honor Code. By the nature of the person's age and experience, a plebe is bound to behave differently and have a different frame of reference than a senior or first classman. And so the way West Point implements the Honor Code—that is, effects the disciplinary aspects of it—has to be tempered by some kind of judgment that can be applied to the scales . . . something that takes into consideration the maturity and experience of the cadet involved. The exercise of this judgment is embodied in a system that sets forth the administration and implementation of the Honor Code.

One of the things I did as commandant was to work hard at educating cadets (and officers as well) to understand and accept that it made good sense to exercise understanding and judgment when we were prosecuting violators of the Honor Code, just as we did with the ordinary rules and regs that entered into the examples I cited in chapter 1. This is, of course, a contradiction to the general perception of the Honor Code as having only a single sanction: you violate it, and you're gone.

Under the superintendent's discharge authority, a cadet who has committed an honor violation can be allowed to enlist in the regular army and serve for a year or more. Then if performance and conditions warrant, the cadet may be allowed to return to the Academy. We've advanced to that level.

I use the word *advanced* advisedly because I believe that this policy represents the right thing to do—in very specific and rare circumstances. I don't mean to imply, nor do I believe for an instant, that the concept of honor at West Point has been weakened or diminished by this policy. It hasn't. But if you try to fit each case of individual behavior into a rigid pattern—with no room for facts that could never be anticipated—you will lose more in undeveloped talent than you could ever gain in lessons learned.

It takes strong leadership to implement and exercise policies like this, but in the long run, it will produce better leaders from the young people who are exposed to this kind of treatment. Said another way, if you paint with too broad a brush, you can't draw the finest lines and you're bound to make mistakes. A lighter, more thoughtful touch is sometimes warranted, and when properly applied, the results are worth far more than the extra effort and risk involved.

> ★ ★ ★
>
> **If you try to fit each case of individual behavior into a rigid pattern—with no room for facts that could never be anticipated—you will lose more in undeveloped talent than you could ever gain in lessons learned.**

Here's an example: Let's say there's a plebe, fresh out of high school where he was surrounded by other young men and women who weren't exactly the world's most serious students. Many of them used crib notes, cheated on tests, and generally failed to put forth their best effort. Or perhaps, this plebe was raised in an impoverished area—in a less-affluent rural setting or a crime-ridden section of the inner city.

The point is this: he's spent the formative years of his life in a place where adults weren't particularly attentive to his behavior—good or bad. They let him slide. He's been surrounded by drugs, crime, poverty, whatever. Sound like high school students in many parts of the United States today? I'm sure it does, and it sends a strong message to everyone in the business of developing leaders from this group of young men and women.

Despite all of the vicissitudes that can affect the behavior of students in these situations, there are many who somehow surmount these obstacles and make it into West Point. Clearly, the men and women who have accomplished something like that possess an inner strength that is worth supporting and nurturing. Their road to the Academy has been far bumpier than the road traveled by, say, someone who grew up in relative opulence and attended the finest prep schools.

So we keep in mind that no one arrives at West Point as an empty vessel, and though the young cadets who have had to overcome extraordinary life circumstances may be highly motivated and ambitious, they may also be lacking in some of the skills required for success in this far more rigid and demanding environment. Simply put, there are things they will not pick up right away, and that includes at least some of the basic tenets of the Honor Code.

Now I know some people would argue that honor is a black-and-white issue, but I can say from long experience that, as with duty, there is more than one shade of gray. Shortly before I arrived as commandant, there was a cadet who had exercised poor judgment a few days before graduation and was held over for possible disciplinary action. He had used a written authorization that he had found on the ground to obtain a privilege he was not authorized to have. He did not steal the authorization or obtain it by wrongful means; he simply stumbled across it one day while walking around the Academy grounds. The honorable thing—the harder right—would have been to pick up this piece of paper and turn it over to a senior officer, so that it would be returned to its rightful owner. Unfortunately, this cadet chose to use the paper to gain something that was not rightfully his and enjoy certain privileges he would not otherwise have had during his final days at the Academy.

I know some people would argue that honor is a black-and-white issue, but I can say from long experience that, as with duty, there is more than one shade of gray.

His act of misrepresentation was inevitably revealed, and he was charged with violating the Honor Code. Should he have been discharged from the Academy for such a transgression? Clearly his sense of right and wrong—*What's the honorable thing to do?*—was not fully formed, and that was disappointing at the very least. Compounding matters, he was a senior and should have known better.

Still, the Academy faced a dilemma in this case. Four years had been invested in this young man. Did it make sense to kick him out, on the eve of graduation, for using something to his advantage that he was not authorized to have?

Yes.

While the cadet's transgression on the surface may have appeared trivial, if you weigh other factors (most notably his age, experience, and familiarity with the rules and expectations of the Academy), you can see that the offense had to be viewed much more seriously. Cadets are expected to know in their hearts (and heads) the difference between right and wrong, and to choose accordingly. And if his record is exemplary? Well, you might think that would be an extenuating circumstance, one that would be viewed in his favor. Wrong. An older cadet with a nearly perfect record is held to the highest of standards. A senior is much more likely than a plebe to face harsh disciplinary measures. If you're a plebe, you're considered a work in progress; mistakes are inevitable. If you're a senior, though, you ought to know better, and you will suffer the consequences if, after all that training, you don't. It's almost inconceivable that a cadet could reach that level and still be capable of such poor behavior and judgment.

Complicated, isn't it? Fortunately and wisely, the Academy (with the full approval of the army's senior leadership) has created disciplinary measures that provide the superintendent with alternatives to simple discharge. The point is not to lower the standard but to make sure that the standard is upheld fairly and reasonably, and sometimes compassionately (another principle I discuss later in this book).

One of the more interesting books I've read in past years is *Lying: Moral Choice in Public and Private Life*. Elegantly written by Sissela Bok, wife of former Harvard University president Derek Bok, the book is a thoughtful and educated treatise on lying, an act that obviously represents a fundamental violation of the West Point Honor Code. And yet the author argues effectively and passionately that in some cases, lying is not the overtly dishonorable act it is thought to be. In fact, on some occasions it may be a perfectly reasonable and human thing to do. Consider the so-called *white lie,* which is often intended not to gain something favorable for the one who lies but rather to protect the feelings of someone else.

Let's say you receive a phone call from a friend who has just bought a dog that he and his wife are crazy about. He tells you all about this wonderful dog, but you are not all that enthusiastic about the breed, perhaps having had a bad experience of your own. So you listen politely, and when he inevitably asks how you like his dog, you tell him that they are certainly good dogs and you are especially glad he and his wife have found theirs to be such a good pet.

The truth is, of course, that you do not like this breed, yet you refrain from saying so. That's not really the whole truth, is it? Sure, it's just a harmless white lie, a very small and benign lie but a lie, nonetheless. Have you violated the Honor Code? Or was this the sensitive, thoughtful thing to do? How would your friend have felt if you told him, "You know, I just don't care for dogs like yours at all"?

★ ★ ★

The principles we're discussing in this book are a good road map for helping leaders reach the right conclusions. But the answers aren't always easy to ascertain, especially when you discover that there is more than one "right" answer.

White lies exist on the periphery of the realm we refer to as honorable behavior—of choosing the harder right instead of the easier wrong. For many of us, it's hard to tell a white lie, but is a white lie the right thing when it means you'll avoid hurting someone else? In my way of thinking, a white lie under the right conditions can reflect honorable behavior. This is just another example of the challenge of leadership, of mastering the art of balance, and understanding that strength does not mean unwavering rigidity. The older I get and the more experience I acquire, the more I realize that every situation and every person deserve to be examined individually with the best effort I can afford. The principles we're discussing in this book are a good road map for helping leaders reach the right conclusions. But the answers aren't always easy to ascertain, especially when we discover that there is more than one right answer.

THE HONOR CODE IN ACTION

Let's look for a moment at how the Honor Code is implemented. Cadets charged with an Honor Code violation are judged by a jury of their peers. They must first answer to an honor committee comprised of other cadets. The committee reviews the case, then makes a recommendation to the commandant, who can recommend various levels of punishment to the superintendent. As in any jury trial, the commandant or superintendent wouldn't mete out a more severe sentence than that recommended by the committee, but they can reduce or mediate the recommended sentence. That is, instead of expulsion, the commandant might elect to recommend a second chance, an option of a stint in the regular army, for example, followed by a possible return to the Academy. The superintendent can approve or direct that the sentence be carried out as recommended by the honor committee.

The option of a second chance is rare, but it is an option. I think that kind of larger view—I don't like to call it flexibility because that carries the negative implication that morality can be flexible, which it really can't—can be beneficial. A leader must exercise strength and wisdom when making tough decisions, but common sense comes in handy too. I had a teacher in high school—

a wonderful, old southern gentleman—who loved to recite poetry. He'd stand in front of the class and read to us in a mellifluous voice, and afterward he'd lower his text, smile, and say, "Boys, how do you know that's poetry?"

In return, he'd get mostly blank stares.

"Well, boys," he'd say, "you just . . . know."

Similarly, how do you know when something is honorable or not? Well, like the teacher said, you just . . . know. Granted, you don't know from the moment you become a human being or from the moment you set foot on the grounds of the U.S. Military Academy, and you realize at some point that you don't even know all of it when you become an officer. It's a sense that ripens over time.

Schweitzer was right: ethics is our way of being human. That means that sometimes you don't turn your back on a person even though there is a paragraph in the rule book that says the offense is punishable by discharge. And that's part of being a leader. You're going to be the person who makes the tough decision, the life-changing decision, so you have to know in your heart whether a specific transgression represents such a breach of honorable behavior that it cannot be tolerated.

HONOR: AT WEST POINT AND IN THE PRIVATE SECTOR

Sometimes the harsh realities of life can intrude on the decision-making process and make a complicated process even more complicated. I arrived as a cadet at West Point in 1951, fresh on the heels of a famous—or infamous—cheating scandal. During the spring of that year, a specially appointed board of officers had reviewed the allegations, most of which focused on the football team. The board understood that at least a few members of the class of 1951 were involved. And yet graduation took place as scheduled, and no seniors were dismissed. Instead, punishment was meted out to underclassmen. The actual violations involved a very small number of young men, but a great many others were at least to some extent aware of the violations. In the end, eleven cadets were found to have cheated, and seventy-nine others were found guilty of tolerating the cheating. All ninety were expelled from the Academy. But every single member of the class of 1951 was allowed to graduate. Why? I would have to say, looking with the advantage of historical perspective, that the board of officers was faced with a number of difficult choices, including the practicality of the immediate situation. The Korean War was escalating, and officers were needed in the field; these young men were available and prepared to serve. As it happened, many of those newly commissioned officers went straight into combat, with little training beyond what they had received at the Academy, and some were killed in action. In fact, many of those who were dismissed simply enlisted in the army and also served, often with distinction, and some of them were also killed in action.

So who in the broadest sense violated the concept of honor in this case? The cadets who cheated? The members of the board of officers who decided to overlook some of their violations? Did they not also choose the easier wrong? I find this to be an issue that can be argued on both sides. History is replete with these kinds of examples because we're talking about a subject that in so many instances has no clear lines that mark its boundaries. You could obviously say that if you tell a lie, purposely, to deceive and promote your own interests, you've violated the concept of honor. That's correct. And obvious. You're smack in the middle of the target on that one. You're not out on the edges, where it can be far more difficult to ascertain right from wrong.

I don't mean to imply that honor is in any way a concept that has been lost, at least not at West Point or in the army. But in the civilian world, especially in the business community, the answer is perhaps less clear. Leaders in the business world are almost universally the ones who have demonstrated an ability to make money. That's important because when you boil it down to its essence, the critical mission in business—the mandate—is to use the resources of your company to make money. The purpose of the company will be charted in different words, involving as it must the production of goods or services to fulfill a higher purpose. Obviously, you don't make money just by making money. In the private sector, ideally, you create something that contributes to the common good, which then builds a profit, and earns money to do more for the common good. In all candor, however, the idea that someone must be an honorable person in order to successfully run a business . . . well, that isn't necessarily built into the equation. Unfortunately, in the business world as opposed to the military, we tend to know less about the ethics of the person in charge because too often we're not interested in testing the whole person. We look at only one aspect of his character: *Does he produce? Does he have the vision to run this business so it can make a profit?* When you look at some of the more distressing examples of immoral business behavior—Enron, Tyco, WorldCom, and the like—you begin to understand the flaw inherent in this type of philosophy. Experience shows that, ultimately, the people running these companies and making enormous profits begin to feel bulletproof, as if the accepted standards of right and wrong no longer apply to them.

I don't think this happens very often, if ever, in the military, in part because financial gain is not part of the formula. Salaries are generally modest by corporate standards; furthermore, they are listed in the law and so are public knowledge. Moreover, the entire point of the military is to "protect and serve," and to that end an enormous amount of time is devoted to training and teaching those who will sooner or later follow in the footsteps of today's leaders.

In the business world, it's almost the opposite: *I'm not training that guy to take my place!* I don't mean to denigrate the many fine men and women who are leaders in the business world; there are plenty of talented, thoughtful corporate leaders. By and large, they are measured by very exacting standards, but I think it's fair to say that they're not all measured by standards that include the rigorous concepts of honor we've been discussing here. I don't have a magic bullet to offer, but it's a shame.

ETHICS AND BUSINESS

And so the problem in the private sector is that there really isn't any measure that respects and rewards honesty. Oh sure, we pay lip service to it. We have ethics programs, and most employees—especially at the management level—are trained to respect the concepts of honor and dignity, and almost all of them do. Interestingly enough, though, the more you try to instill these concepts and beliefs, the less likely they are to be sincerely embraced. The training becomes just another thing to endure: *Oh, great. Ethics training this week. Hope I can stay awake.* It almost seems as though the minute it becomes part of a formula, the less important it becomes—just another thing to be checked off and forgotten as the pursuit of profit (the real goal) continues.

That just doesn't work. Honor, and the demand for honorable behavior, is not the kind of thing that can be shoved aside and still be of any use. It has to be integral to what you do, day in and day out. It's a behavioral philosophy that must be implemented and repeatedly modeled from the top. Of course, for that to happen, there must be some assurance that the right people reach the top; as leaders are promoted through the system, consideration should be given to factors beyond intelligence, ambition, and business acumen. Integrity must be recognized as a prerequisite. Granted, integrity and honorable behavior are not easily measured. But if they're part of the formula used to select leaders at the highest levels, then we're at least on the right track.

If the selection process ignores integrity completely, and focuses instead on who made the most money last year, you've got the ingredients of a serious ethical problem. Why? Because it encourages cutting corners. Bonuses and raises are meted out on the basis of performance, and performance is measured in revenues, profits, and stock prices. Human nature being what it is, people will often gravitate toward the boundaries rather than the center of acceptable behavior, especially when they can create numbers that put more money in their own pockets.

Some people would argue that this is the way the game is played. Some games are called football; some are called soccer. This one is called business, and these are the rules of the game. But from a human standpoint, you have to ask yourself, *Do I really feel good about the way I'm playing the game?* Having lived the life I've lived, if I thought any of my subordinates or employees were behaving dishonorably—in other words, trying to lie, cheat, or steal something—I would not tolerate their presence, period. That sounds—high-minded and harsh, but there is no other way to lead effectively, either in the military or in business.

If the selection process ignores integrity completely, and focuses instead on who made the most money last year, you've got the ingredients of a serious ethical problem. Why? Because it encourages cutting corners.

It saddens me sometimes to think that the concept of honorable behavior has fallen out of favor. Sure, my background is unique; I'm a military man, a combat veteran, but as such I am no stranger to the harsh realities of life. And yet, there is something eternally noble about the outlook of Henry Stimson, who was our secretary of war in World War II. Early in the war, there was considerable discussion about how the Allied forces were going to obtain information about the plans of the enemy. Stimson's reaction to the concept of espionage was to rather famously proclaim his disinterest in stealing Japanese or German code because, as he put it, "Gentlemen do not read each other's mail." In light of current world affairs, such decorum seems a painfully quaint and archaic sentiment. Both warfare and business have gone through enormous transformations since the middle of the twentieth century. That's simply a fact that can't be denied or overlooked. Stimson was a fine man, and I always admired him for his insistence on playing by the rules. But those rules, particularly in matters of national defense, do not and cannot exist today.

A legitimate aspect of business, as with the military, is ferreting out other people's secrets, and that in itself has some impact on our view of what constitutes right and wrong: *How far can we go? Are there limits?* Strong, ethical leaders understand in their hearts and heads that the dogged pursuit of success and a keen desire to defeat the competition don't mean all bets are off. Granted, there is a different structure in the business world than there is in the military, but the concept of honorable behavior still applies. And there are consequences for behaving dishonorably.

Here's an interesting story—again with a few details altered—that speaks to precisely this issue. The central figure of this incident was a senior executive of a very large, successful company that had a number of lucrative contracts with the U.S. Government. It was quite common for representatives of the government to visit the site where the company's work was being done.

Well after one such visit, it was discovered that a government official had inadvertently left behind a package that contained a small but confidential piece of information. The package eventually made its way into the hands of a junior executive, who apparently did not grasp the full implications of using the information to the company's advantage. And even when the responsible senior executive discovered this transgression, he did not take immediate and appropriate action. Why? Hard to say, although it was clear that he should have realized that his company would obtain an improper and immediate benefit from this information. Subsequently, when the situation came to light, the government took the predictable step of not only canceling current contracts but also disqualifying the company from bidding on any future contracts. Not surprisingly, the senior executive was discharged from his position, a sad and stark fall from grace for a man who had been widely viewed as a candidate for larger roles in the company.

Strong, ethical leaders understand in their hearts and heads that the dogged pursuit of success and a keen desire to defeat the competition don't mean all bets are off.

This is a telling example of failing to live up to the equivalent of the West Point Honor Code, of tolerating dishonorable behavior. Moreover, it was a vivid example of the U.S. government imposing rigid guidelines on the business community, where honor can be a shifty concept: *These are our standards, and you're working for us. Even though you're a private business, this is what we expect.* I consider that a valuable lesson for leaders in the world of commercial business. Competition is fine. It's healthy and necessary in a capitalist society. But there are rules and expectations, and you violate them at your own risk.

I am certain that my experience at West Point, where a sense of honor was ingrained, helped me to become a better person and a more effective and ethical leader. I'm not saying that everything I learned at the Academy applies word for word to the business world.

But the fact that a template of honor was part of my makeup when I joined the business world was a significant advantage. Lacking that template, I would have found myself rather unsure about the shading of certain ethical boundaries.

As it happened, I had a fairly well-developed sense of what I considered to be honorable and proper behavior, and I did my best to apply that philosophy to running the business that paid my salary. It wasn't that I felt compelled to disagree with everyone, or to accuse coworkers of dishonorable behavior; rather, the confidence I gained as a military officer (interestingly enough) allowed me to question the behavior and practices around me. Rather than saying, "You're wrong!" I'd say, "Tell me why you feel this method is right." In that way, we could learn from each other, which is always the most constructive approach to solving problems and changing attitudes.

One might think that the military, where the stakes are so high, would be a place where honorable behavior is often sacrificed in the pursuit of a higher goal. But as someone who has spent a lot of time in both the U.S. Army and the private sector, I can say with great confidence that this is not the case. Indeed, the bottom-line mentality so pervasive in the business community, coupled with a tendency to turn a blind eye to such transgressions, makes the private sector a far more ambiguous place, morally and ethically speaking.

★ ★ ★

Somehow, the workforce must feel invested in the company—at all levels. They have to care about more than their income and retirement packages. They have to care about each other and, in so doing, care about the image of their company as well. In the military, that's part and parcel of what we do: foster teamwork.

Typically, the man or woman who can figure out how to make money is the most important and richly rewarded person in an organization. As I've already noted, it doesn't work that way in the military. Everyone who does his or her job gets promoted; men and women receive the same increase in pay. Incentive is the reward of knowing that the job was well done, increasing responsibility dictates promotion, and both depend on the skills individuals bring to their duties. Most important of all, in the military, we all live together and work together, which not only helps create the sense that we're on a common mission but also encourages a sense of community.

A leader who can reproduce this atmosphere in the private sector, I believe, will have a far greater chance of success, although I would be the first to admit that this is no small task. A company Christmas party isn't enough. Somehow, the workforce must feel invested in the company—at all levels. They have to care about more than their income and retirement packages. They have to care about each other and, in so doing, care about the image of their company as well. In the military, that's part and parcel of what we do: foster teamwork. In the private sector, intense competition between coworkers is often standard operating procedure because the winner can earn a bonus or promotion and higher pay. I'm not saying that competition is a bad thing; I just think it's important for a leader to recognize that internal competition has a tendency to pull the community apart.

And when all is said and done, if you're a leader in the army, in business, or in the not-for-profit world, the time will come when you will be faced with this dilemma: to compromise your principles or take the (possibly unpleasant) consequences. What will you do? Will you choose the harder right or the easier wrong? In the most basic sense, this is where you call on the principles of leadership and measure yourself as a person of honor.

3

FAITH

*If you're in charge, let the master carpenter do the wood-
work . . . and don't forget that Jesus was a carpenter.*
—THE AUTHOR

*F**aith* is an interesting word. It has gained considerable attention
in recent years and is sometimes seen as the first step down a
slippery slope, often invoking the concept of a supreme being in a
rigorous religious setting. Personally, I like the word and the concept
and take comfort in hearing it used in so many contexts—secular
and nonsecular. While I have my own feelings and beliefs about religion and its place in my life, I am a staunch advocate of tolerance
and diversity; and I think that is a requisite for good leadership in
today's world. Human as we are, it's natural for us to have faith in
something or someone greater than ourselves. While I do ask God
for help, mostly I thank Him, many times a day, for all I have and
all I am able to do with it.

I think that's an important element of leadership because, after
all, virtually everything we do is based on an act of faith. Think
about it: in order to live a life with meaning and purpose (and isn't
that what any leader strives to do?), you have to acknowledge and
accept that you are not the center of the universe. There has to be
something deep inside, a little voice that says, *I'm doing this because
there is something larger at stake, and I'm just one piece of a bigger picture. It's not all about me. I have to do my job the best I can because
it's essential to our mission. The bigger picture is beyond my control.*

But I have faith that when I do my job, it's going to work into this bigger picture. I can't dictate or control that, but if I do my job well, the right things are going to happen.

FAITH IN YOUR COUNTRY AND YOUR MISSION

Each of us has to define the parameters of that bigger picture and find our own place within the framework. For cadets at the Military Academy, faith quickly becomes a way of life. The motto of the Academy is *Duty, Honor, Country.* In the military, we can make that translation very directly because our primary purpose is to learn all we can in order to serve our country as well, and as faithfully, as we can. We are in the military because we embrace those same ideals espoused at West Point. That means implicitly that we have faith that our country is going to do the right thing. I'm not talking about blind faith—far from it, actually, since the young men and women who come to West Point are among the brightest and most inquisitive of their generation. They come with an innate sense of right and wrong that challenges those things that don't seem right to them. But they also have a desire to serve their country, and as such they are continually building and internalizing their faith in the freedoms upon which our country was founded.

The overarching example of the importance of this faith exists today in the Middle East. There is great controversy with conflicting opinions and attitudes surrounding the United States' military involvement in Iraq. We are at war, and the people we're fighting are clearly bent on the destruction of America and the rest of the Western world. In the pursuit of their goals, they are willing to use the most unscrupulous and despicable acts ever visited on their fellow humans.

Whatever your politics and prejudices, the fact is that we're in Iraq, so let's think about our soldiers, marines, airmen, and sailors—

the men and women who put their lives on the line every day to bring freedom and democracy to the people there. Then let's think about their officers and noncommissioned officers who are responsible for leading them in the unprecedented actions of this fight. These dedicated volunteers and their leaders have two choices: they can be bitter and question their service and the leadership above them, or they can faithfully serve their leaders, our country, and the assignments given them. The military men and women and their leaders, in and out of Iraq, believe they are in the service of our country for a purpose. Their faith is the basis of their volunteer service, and they demonstrate that faith every day as they literally risk their lives to bring order out of the chaos they are confronting.

So if you're a young officer in Iraq, fresh out of West Point, the success of your leadership and the survival of your subordinates depend on having faith in your mission—having a belief that you are there for a reason, that there is a higher purpose for the risks you are taking and the hard work you are doing. That's real faith, and it works miracles for the leaders who carry it inside them and inspire their subordinates to do the same.

Faith is also about being able to look in the mirror and say with confidence and certainty, "I believe what my leaders are telling me, and the reasons for doing what I am doing are right and good." In the complex swirl of violence amidst dizzying political conflicts, it's not always possible for leaders on the ground to define those reasons with total clarity. The burden falls on leaders at every level to communicate their faith to those under their command. From the last rung of the ladder to the top, everyone has to have faith in their mission.

In America, we are fortunate to have an educated people who understand intuitively that faith goes beyond country and flag to the foundation of the republic itself. Faith has to do with people being free to weigh what they see and decide for themselves; it has to do with something called *democracy,* in which you can do what you want as long as there is no restriction against it. That's a world apart from a system that allows you to do only what those in power may allow you to do. People's rights have no standing in those systems, and we downplay the meaning of their attacks on us (on 9/11 and many times before) at our own peril.

FAITH IN OUR LEADERS

I would also argue that faith can be a difficult thing to define. Benjamin Franklin believed that the most important function of any human being was to please his fellow man; by doing good for others, he would be doing good in the eyes of God. Others, who have a picture in their minds of a specific higher power, might question that philosophy. Faith, then, is not something that you can bring to the table and say, "Aha, here it is! It measures two feet on this side, three feet on that side, and it will always be in this place when you want to find it." Nevertheless, faith, while amorphous, is an essential part of leadership. And there are times—tough times—when people will not understand what's happening, and they're going to need help and guidance, something they can lean on. That's when a leader has to be able to communicate and indoctrinate others with faith. Leaders must be able to stand up and convince the followers: "We're going to be okay, folks. Just have faith. We'll get the job done, and everything will work out."

Granted, sometimes you have to elaborate; you can't do it with bluster or by giving an unconvincing story to the troops (or to the employees in your office). They're too smart for that, and they deserve far better treatment from a leader. The truth is they don't always want or need a detailed explanation, which is why a legitimate element of leadership is faith—faith that the people in charge know what they are doing and that they, in turn, have faith in the mission. It's common sense, really. Think about it. If you felt the man you were following had no faith in what he was doing . . . if you were plagued by a nagging sense of doubt about his level of commitment . . . then surely this would have an impact on your performance. How do you follow him if you don't know what he stands for?

Faith is a sensitive word and, for some, can even be inflammatory: it evokes thoughts and images of morality and religion. Too often it tends to be a divisive term—*are you a Christian or Muslim or Jew?*—when it should be a term that brings us together. When I speak of faith, especially as it pertains to leadership, I'm trying to convey something else entirely—something that followers can feel, that these people whom you are leading have complete faith in what they are doing.

So the obvious question is, "What inspires that sense of trust . . . that *faith*?" Again, there's more than one answer. It might be faith in the mission, the country, the commanding officer. But for any organization to succeed and thrive, there must be faith. Sometimes it's at a very low and personal level: "The lieutenant said the chow truck would be here to feed us before we moved out, and I'm sticking right here because that's what he said."

And he stays, and the chow truck arrives, and he believes even more in his leaders. That's faith, and that's how it's created and nurtured.

Subordinates have to be able to feel this faith and translate it into something of personal value, something they can use. Rest assured this is not a passive thing. There is an acting out that's part of it: faith moves people to action, and it does, in my experience, involve morality. Simply put, when leaders command the faith of a group, it demonstrates that they have been able to convince their followers that they have a moral compass. If they lack this fundamental mechanism, in my opinion, leaders and their followers are doomed to fail. There is a simple element of trust involved, something that makes an employee look at his boss and listen to his words and decide, "I believe him." Lacking that trust . . . that *faith* . . . a leader faces an insurmountable uphill climb.

How does a leader demonstrate that he is worthy of such trust? Well, accumulated experience, of course, is part of it. With any new leader, there are doubts, so it helps if he has the right background—if, as a prime example, he comes from a place like West Point. At the Academy, our most important job is to develop the capability to inspire that trust and the respect that goes with it. We work on it every day, and it has grown stronger with every one of the two hundred years of the Academy's existence. It's validated by senior officers who come back to tell us what the young lieutenants are like; they invariably give high marks to the West Pointers, who form a vital part of the army's leadership at every level.

So the youngsters who are part of today's army (and the older sergeants as well) come to expect that the newly commissioned officers from West Point with whom they serve are going to have well-developed skills; despite youth and comparative inexperience, they carry a certain gravitas. When these young lieutenants give an order, their troops can trust that they know what they're talking about. They have a faith that runs between the leader and the led. Again, this is not a blind faith—that's not something I would try to communicate because there's an important distinction. This type of faith is precisely the opposite of blind faith. It's studied and informed. We know where this lieutenant was trained, we've watched him carefully, and we've made a determination that he is worthy of our service and respect.

We have faith in him.

There are times, of course, when a leader will feel uncertainty, and that's where the moral compass takes center stage. If you want to be a leader, it's inevitable: eventually you are going to find yourself in uncharted waters. What do you depend on then? Your faith—faith in yourself and faith in the system. And then you have to find a way to communicate that faith to your subordinates. That is one of the most challenging components of leadership: the ability to translate your faith to those under your command.

FAITH IN GOD

For the purposes of this book, I've taken the West Point motto and replaced the word *country* with the word *faith*. For our soldiers, faith and country are intertwined. We defend our country. That is a soldier's duty. But in terms of leadership, we're really talking about faith. It's often been said that when soldiers are in combat, they aren't thinking about service to the country. It becomes something much simpler, much more personal and human. The soldier thinks about defending his buddies: *I'm fighting for the guy on my left and the guy on my right.* To me, that's the most basic translation of faith.

In the course of time, there are some things that can't easily be explained, and this, too, is where faith comes into play. I relate this next piece of my personal history because I have no explanation for it. Near the end of my training in Ranger School, I spent a period of time in the mountains of northern Georgia. This was in the winter months, and the conditions were pretty bleak with ice, snow, wind, and rain most all the time.

One evening we were out on patrol, and as usual, I was one of two men walking point. (Point means just that—you are at the "point of the spear," the first man to place footprints in the path where your patrol will walk.) We did this on the buddy system, and the point men usually were pretty good with a compass and could get the troops through in the dark or in bad weather. Well, it was long after midnight, and we were moving along a narrow trail on a steep slope in a battlefield infiltration exercise, operating against troops from the infantry division at Fort Benning. They were designated the "aggressors," and we were assigned the task of getting behind their lines to destroy a strategic target: a large dam on a local river. As we were going along the trail, I saw movement that indicated there were troops ahead in the distance. I knew they would be able to sense our motion if we continued on the trail. So I turned and signaled to everyone: get off the side of the trail! Then I took a big jump myself, which wasn't very wise since I was literally surrounded by the blackest darkness imaginable. It turned out that I stepped off the trail and into nothing. I can remember vividly the feeling of air beneath my feet, of falling like a stone with no control over my body. I remember clutching my rifle as I did a slow rotation in the air, almost like a big cartwheel . . . and then I remember landing. Well, not landing, really, but hitting something and then sliding . . . all the way down a steep, rocky slope, probably thirty feet or more. And suddenly there I was—upright, on two feet, still holding my rifle.

★ ★ ★

When soldiers are in combat, they aren't thinking about service to the country. It becomes something much simpler, much more personal and human. The soldier thinks about defending his buddies: *I'm fighting for the guy on my left and the guy on my right.*

Not only was I not seriously injured, but I also didn't feel any pain whatsoever. No broken bones, no torn ligaments, not even a scrape. How could that have happened? My personal belief—the only explanation that makes any sense whatsoever—is that God intervened. His hand just reached in and guarded me from physically hurting myself. It wasn't as if the rocks turned to rubber or the air turned to water so I didn't fall fast. There was nothing quite as obvious as that. But *something* happened, and to this day I can remember standing there for a moment, turning around, with the rifle in my hand, looking for the rest of the patrol, which had scrambled down a gentler part of the slope. And then we were all together again. No one even commented on it because it was so dark they couldn't see it. I didn't say anything either. But in my mind, I couldn't help but wonder how I had survived. There had to be something involved, something beyond pure, dumb luck. God had other plans for me.

I believed then, and I certainly believe now, that there really is a God who looks out for all of us. That is part of my faith. It's a belief in someone or something that can't be readily or easily explained. Why is this important? Well, I think it speaks to a person's character—a person of faith is someone who looks beyond himself, who understands that he is part of something larger than he is able to describe precisely or comprehend fully.

Here's an intriguing piece of West Point history: there was a time when religious service was mandatory for cadets at West Point; however, this practice was phased out sometime before my tenure as commandant. This happened in the seventies when the country was experiencing great turmoil and generational conflict, a by-product of which was a ferocious individualism and a tendency to mistrust any type of bureaucracy, including the bureaucracies that oversaw organized religion. This flowed down to the military, at least to the extent that it was deemed inappropriate to force people to attend religious services. The Protestant, Jewish, and Catholic chaplains at West Point were among my close friends, and when I arrived, I asked them how they felt about cadets no longer being required to attend church. I was concerned and wanted their counsel; their reaction was enlightening. Reverend Dick Camp, our Protestant cadet chaplain, spoke for all of them. "As chaplain," he said calmly, "I have to agree with that."

Surprised almost to the point of speechlessness, I could only ask, "Why?"

"Because," he said with a smile, "if people are being forced to come in here and listen to me preach, I don't think they're going to get as much out of it. It will be a lot better if they come because they want to."

I had to agree with his calm logic, of course. At the same time, I couldn't help but feel (and I still do) that the exercising of one's religious faith is an integral piece of the training to become a leader. It's about being part of a community, and it's about duty: I have to get up on Sunday morning and go to church. The anecdotes heard in church or temple are important . . . anecdotes about faith, leadership, love, selflessness. So I do believe that organized religious services represent a superb educational tool for a leader. That said, Dick Camp clearly steered me against mandating religious service—the reasons he cited then are the same today as they were those many years ago. We believe in our freedoms, and it's surely better to leave the freedom of such choices in the hands of the individual.

All leadership, in essence, is an act of faith.

Interestingly enough, a significant number of cadets at West Point today enthusiastically embrace their religions. Many still go to chapel every day. And while the Academy remains overwhelmingly Christian (and predominantly Catholic), there are significant numbers of other faiths: Mormons, Jews, and Muslims as well. What's happened—and I think this is a very healthy development—is that the cadets have taken it upon themselves to organize religious groups and gatherings and to support each other in the pursuit of their faith—however that faith might be exercised. It's something they've decided on their own as opposed to something that has been foisted upon them. As such, I think it plays an important role in building leaders at West Point. These young men and women, officers in training, have decided on their own to actively profess their faith and to communicate that faith to others. They are, as I often announce to whomever is within earshot, America's next greatest generation. When all is said and done, they are the ones who will lead the defenders of our country through this deadly war against the terrorists who would destroy our freedoms and our way of life.

All leadership, in essence, is an act of faith. When I was a battalion commander during the Vietnam War, I learned late in my tour of duty that my replacement's arrival had been delayed. Normal army procedure was for a soldier to leave precisely on the date of his estimated return from overseas (DEROS in troop lingo). I was free to go; however, my battalion had been preparing for operations in Cambodia, and suddenly I realized that they would be left without a commander for at least several weeks if I left on schedule.

By this time I'd been in the army for fifteen years, so I knew instinctively that this wasn't right. Here's a battalion going into combat, and the battalion commander is going home? Not a chance. Unless they ordered me to go home, I was staying. And I didn't think that would happen. In fact, while it was proffered to me as a choice—"Time's up; you're free to go"—I'm quite sure my superior officers were enormously relieved that I was willing to stay. More than that, actually, I *wanted* to stay.

So we went into Cambodia, at a time (1970) when Cambodia was one of the most dangerous places in Southeast Asia. We were combat engineers, which meant our secondary mission was to fight as infantry. Our first mission, as we liked to say, was to build the bridges that the infantry crossed in order to attack. We'd say this rather facetiously since by definition the engineers were always among the first to arrive when the army moved into new territory.

In the Vietnam era, the combat engineers would go into the jungles to blow down the trees and quickly lay out a landing zone so the infantry could come in by helicopter. In reality, our engineering capabilities in those circumstances were limited. We were combat soldiers first, engineers second.

Cambodia was a tough place to be around at the time—the Viet Cong had reestablished a foothold after the Tet Offensive, and any battalion entering the region was sure to see intense fighting. In every sense of the word, this assignment required an act of faith. It's quite a thing to stand up in front of a group of young soldiers to describe this assignment: "You're going to board a helicopter and fly into an area you've never seen before—an area thick with enemy soldiers (we know that because some of our aircraft have already been shot down), and once we're on the ground we're going to go to work building landing zones for the big helos and the infantry."

I was fortunate to have an officer commanding our lead company who had been a cadet at West Point while I was an instructor, so we had developed a rapport. I had faith in the mission, and he had faith in me. And together we were able to communicate that faith to the troops. We were successful on that mission and didn't lose one soldier. Things don't always work out so well when you can't control all the variables, but we kept our faith, and our faith brought us all back alive.

GREAT LEADERSHIP, GREAT FAITH

My experience at West Point was critical to the development of this faith. A plebe at the U.S. Military Academy is little more than raw material. Even though they do possess something unusual in terms of ambition and character, at this early stage they are raw material nonetheless. Four years later they emerge as officers who have the capability and the desire to lead . . . trained and educated in an inspirational environment, catching leadership and embracing the formal instruction that we use in teaching leadership. Each day, sometimes overtly but more often subtly, cadets are developing the ability to look at something and say, "Yeah, I've got faith that it's going to work." Or to look at a superior officer and say, "Because of what I know about him, I have faith in what he says, and I will follow him."

Part of the West Point experience is building a foundation that encourages the growth of young leaders so that when they face unknown situations, they will be supported by their faith—faith in their organization, faith in their superiors, faith in their mission, faith in their equipment—faith in that which surrounds and supports them. It is faith that informs so much of leadership, faith that gives the leaders strength by letting them know they are not alone.

It has been said that there are no atheists in foxholes. To a degree, I think that's true although the faith that propels a soldier into combat and gives him the strength to perform courageously is not necessarily a spiritual faith. Think about it. The common denominator for anyone on the field of battle is fear. Everyone experiences fear regardless of rank, and perhaps the officers in charge experience it more acutely than anyone else. They are concerned not only for their own well-being but also feel even more deeply the responsibility for the lives of those under their command.

Faith plays a major role—no, *the* major role—in managing and controlling fear. Fear can be overwhelming. You're in the unknown, often in darkness; the noise or the silence can be terrifying; and there are shells flying all around you. Maybe you're in a helicopter, live fire is crackling through the fuselage, and you're not sure you can get to the landing zone. While training implants the ability to make decisions and take action, faith guides the instincts that produce those decisions and actions. It's faith that takes over when you're enshrouded by the fog of war.

At no time is leadership, fueled by faith, more important than it is in a jumbled scenario of danger, confusion, injury, and death. Leaders have to step up and make decisions, and whatever those decisions might be, you can be sure that they're taken in the final step as a leap of faith. Leaders must be thinking, *This is how we trained; this is what we're going to do.*

You'd be surprised to learn how often a leader gives an order in the heat of combat, looks around, and finds the troops saying, "No way!" because more experienced subordinates are saying, "There's a better way!" It takes time for subordinates to adjust to a new leader, though in combat it takes a lot less because, naturally, everyone is a lot more focused when life and death are in the balance. A good leader has to be prepared for this situation and be able to adapt to it. That's part of the leadership equation, and it doesn't happen overnight. We'll talk more about that in another chapter.

At no time is leadership, fueled by faith, more important than it is in a jumbled scenario of danger, confusion, injury, and death.

You know, the real world is not just like the movies where the leading man stands up and says, "Let's go!" and everyone jumps up and runs "over the top." It is a rare occasion when a leader can step in one day and inspire that sort of confidence and respect the next. I must tell you here, though, that it has happened in Iraq. Brand-new lieutenants, newly graduated and just out of their basic branch course, have actually showed up one night and led their platoons in the attack the very next day. It happened in Desert Storm, and they did it successfully, which is a great testament to the training these young men and women have received at West Point.

The ability to inspire faith—to have that internal fire that ignites and inspires others—is built into the training at the Academy. I liken it to the idea of the revered coach in athletics, the one about whom it is said, "His players would run through a wall for him." So much of it is about faith. It's not just that the players admire or even love the coach (though that may be true) and, therefore, are willing to do literally anything for him. It's about faith: he inspires them to believe that they can accomplish anything, even the seemingly impossible.

Faith is a bipartisan sentiment too. If you're going to be a leader, you have to have faith—in something. There is no way around that. But the idea that there are liberal or conservative attitudes about how you might exercise faith . . . well, to me, that just doesn't make sense. All of us, regardless of how we feel a mission is best accomplished, can have faith in the mission itself. Leadership is all about bringing the pieces of the puzzle together.

Faith occurs at all levels, and a leader has to think of it in those terms. If you're asking people to complete a mission, you have to understand what it is that gives them faith in the mission. And that might be different things to different people, especially if the mission involves stepping off into the abyss, performing a task that is completely foreign to them. It's natural in that situation for people to question their own ability as well as the logic of the exercise in question.

The leader has to create an atmosphere of faith so that those in the organization believe they can accomplish the mission. It sounds like magic, but it really isn't. Almost anyone can do it if he is willing to try. It's a matter of knowing the job and having faith it can be done (and it might be something you've never done, so you're going to have to convince yourself, which means prepare, study, and practice).

Then you're going to have to turn around and say to those whom you need to convince to follow you, whether under your military command or in your civilian employ, "Here's what we're going to do." And then . . . do it.

Good leaders have the ability to inspire faith in others and not because they're magicians or Superman or anything like that. It's because they've done their homework, they've succeeded in the past, and their track record stands as proof of their ability. People generally want to be led; they want to be inspired. And when they see someone who instills confidence, someone who clearly has faith in what they're doing, people fall willingly in line. Why? Because they are inspired by the same kind of faith.

If you, as the leader, don't believe in the mission—if you lack faith—then you're bound to fail. Sure, Hollywood makes up wonderful stories about the guy who says, "I don't know whether we can do this or not, but we're sure as heck gonna give it a try!" Then everyone cheers and jumps on the bandwagon. But that's not real life. Even though we all have those kinds of doubts and questions from time to time—*Can I really do this? Can I really make it happen?*—it's necessary to have a deep-rooted faith in what we're doing. And the way we develop that is through preparation. I call it "studied acceptance that this is what we're going to do."

Now if I think it's a mission that has great risk associated with it, well, then it's a mission that has great risk associated with it. I just do all I can to try to reduce the risk. But I know in my heart that when the shooting starts, it's likely that someone is not going to come back. I know that, and I can't get away from it. But I have faith that I'm going to do everything I can, everything in my power, to accomplish the mission and bring them all back. That's all I can do. In the end, it's faith that sustains me, and ultimately it sustains everyone who is part of our effort.

It's amazing what faith actually produces—situations that, if you just stepped into them from the outside, would look utterly insane, yet somehow men and women in those situations perform feats of incredible bravery.

You might wonder whether a leader is obligated to share his doubts or candid assessment with those under his command. This is a fair question but one that has no easy answer. As I said, it's vital to project an image of faith, but perhaps not to the point of insulting the intelligence of your subordinates. Projecting confidence is also part of that, and we'll get to that in a later chapter as well. As a battalion commander in combat, I never had a specific conversation with my soldiers or with my company commanders that detailed the likelihood of fatalities on an upcoming mission. My company commanders might have had that conversation with their troops, but I would not have discussed it with them. They were aware of the danger; they didn't need to hear it from me. What they needed from me was reassurance: "Guys, we're all coming home." They all knew there would be casualties, and yet they had faith.

None of us is immune to fear as I've noted, but there was an unspoken faith among soldiers that if something bad happened, it wouldn't happen to them. And even if it did, their buddies would do what had to be done to bring them back, preferably alive. And I'll tell you, it's amazing what faith actually produces—situations that, if you just stepped into them from the outside, would look utterly insane, yet somehow men and women in those situations perform feats of incredible bravery. They do these things because of their training, their preparation, and the inner strength that good leadership imparts.

They do it because they have faith.

4

COURAGE

It takes real courage to admit you're wrong.

—THE AUTHOR

Courage is a slippery concept, at least as difficult to grasp as it is to exercise. We hear it all the time, often in reference to acts that require uncommon physical prowess or nearly impossible feats of endurance. But I believe there are distinctions that must be made, and parameters established, to differentiate between behavior that is courageous (and by definition honorable) and that which is merely foolish or stubborn. The former is part and parcel of good leadership; the latter is a formula for disaster.

It's also important to keep in mind that courage comes in many shapes and sizes—from the type that occasionally results in a Purple Heart or Medal of Honor, to the kind you never hear about: the corporate executive who sits behind a desk and makes a decision that is morally and ethically correct, despite the fact that it places his career and livelihood in jeopardy. Another word often heard in conjunction with courage is *character*. I like to think of character as describing the way one behaves in the dark.

I've heard cancer survivors brush aside the notion that their survival is evidence of courageous behavior, since there was no choice involved. Wrong. There may be degrees of difficulty and shades of gray, but there is always a choice to be made—in this case, to wither and die without a fight, or to accept the rigors of treatment so that you might be around to see your children grow up. That I can tell you from personal experience: I am a cancer survivor.

Let me take a moment here to chronicle the experience of one man, as ordinary as you and me, not large in stature or possessing some uniquely distinguishing features. In other words, he's not visibly marked by some characteristic as one to watch, something we often cite as a factor that portends greatness. My friend and colleague, Colonel Jack Jacobs, U.S. Army (Ret.), is an outstanding example of a man of courage. Colonel Jacobs was commissioned through ROTC at Rutgers University and recently served as a visiting professor of leadership at the U.S. Military Academy. He has had a very successful career in private business, and is also a member of the Council of Foreign Relations. As a first lieutenant in Vietnam, he was awarded our country's highest decoration for valor, the Congressional Medal of Honor. He also holds three Bronze Stars and two Silver Stars. Jack's story is best told by the citation that describes his heroic actions and courage under fire:

CITATION: JACOBS, JACK H.

For conspicuous gallantry and intrepidity in action at the risk of his life above and beyond the call of duty.

Captain Jacobs (then first lieutenant), Infantry, distinguished himself while serving as assistant battalion advisor, 2nd Battalion, 16th Infantry, 9th Infantry Division, Army of the Republic of Vietnam. The 2nd Battalion was advancing to contact when it came under intense heavy machine gun and mortar fire from a Viet Cong battalion positioned in well-fortified bunkers. As the 2nd Battalion deployed into attack formation, its advance was halted by devastating fire. Captain Jacobs, with the command element of the lead company, called for and directed air strikes on the enemy positions to facilitate a renewed attack. Due to the intensity of the enemy fire and heavy casualties to the command group, including the company commander, the attack stopped and the friendly troops became disorganized. Although wounded by mortar fragments, Captain Jacobs assumed command of the allied company, ordered a withdrawal from the exposed position and established a defensive perimeter. Despite profuse bleeding from head wounds which impaired his vision, Captain Jacobs, with complete disregard for his safety, returned under intense fire to evacuate a seriously wounded advisor to the safety of a wooded area where he administered lifesaving first aid. He then returned through heavy automatic weapons fire to evacuate the wounded company commander. Captain Jacobs made repeated trips across the fire-swept open rice paddies evacuating wounded and their weapons. On three separate occasions, Captain Jacobs contacted and drove off Viet Cong squads who were searching for allied wounded and weapons, single-handedly killing three and wounding several others. His gallant actions and extraordinary heroism saved the lives of one U.S. advisor and thirteen allied soldiers. Through his effort the allied company was restored to an effective fighting unit and prevented defeat of the friendly forces by a strong and determined enemy. Captain Jacobs, by his gallantry and bravery in action in the highest traditions of the military service, has reflected great credit upon himself, his unit, and the U.S. Army.

That's an example of courage that jumps off the page at you. But courage comes in all shapes and sizes. The officer who distinguishes himself in the military—first at West Point, and later, perhaps, on the field of battle—is likely to be a courageous and dignified leader in the private sector, should he choose to go that route.

There are behavioral patterns established early in training at the Academy that promote courageous behavior on both a large and small scale. The West Point Honor Code, as earlier noted, demands that all cadets choose the harder right even if that means pointing out the dishonorable behavior of a friend or classmate. This takes courage, and it is a fundamental building block in the creation of a U.S. Army officer.

REACTING TO FEAR

Everyone experiences fear, but some people are more predisposed than others to react to fear courageously. For whatever reason, when the fight-or-flight response kicks in, they are more inclined to fight. I do believe that some of this is innate. Biochemistry and genetics play a role in determining whether we are short or tall, thin or stocky, brilliant or merely competent, so surely they contribute to the anthropological stew that leads one soldier to stand and fight and another to run away. Some people are fighters; some are poets; some are both. That's just the way life works, the hand that nature deals us.

That said, I think it's essential to add that preparation and training can mitigate the dread one naturally experiences when confronted with an obstacle that requires courage to conquer.

Some people are fighters; some are poets; some are both. That's just the way life works, the hand that nature deals us.

COURAGE ON THE BATTLEFIELD

The reality is that no one knows what to expect the first time he goes into battle, nor does one know how he will react. There are expectations and standards, and the degree to which anyone meets those expectations depends largely on two things: training and preparation. Before I stepped foot on my first battlefield, I had decided that I wanted to behave a certain way when that time came, so I prepared to make it as natural as possible to perform certain tasks.

Somewhat to my surprise, I found that when the fighting began and the fog of war kicked in, it came almost naturally to act in the way I had trained. I am not trying to diminish the impact of combat, which some of great experience have called *choreographed insanity.* War is terrifying, gruesome business, and no one walks through it unscathed. But I found that the training I had received gave me the tools to act when and how I needed to.

★ ★ ★

Let's face it—on the battlefield, everybody is scared. Life makes cowards of us all. What defines us is how we respond to life and the challenges it places in front of us.

Simply put, training informs instinct. The survival instinct is powerful indeed, and there is a natural and perfectly reasonable desire to turn and run when the noise is deafening, shells are exploding, and the world seems to be turning upside down. Only through intense training can that instinct be channeled in a positive direction. The goal in training is to teach survival skills that are sometimes antithetical to human nature. You want the soldier to stand and fight to support the mission, but you also want to give him and his unit the greatest chance for survival. Instinct then becomes something different for the trained soldier. He is by nature prepared and intent on carrying out his duties, holding his position, and doing what he has been trained to do.

Let's face it—on the battlefield, everybody is scared. Life makes cowards of us all. What defines us is how we respond to life and the challenges it places in front of us. Every leader must confront circumstances that generate trepidation or even outright fear. Take comfort in knowing that fear is a perfectly reasonable and natural response to these circumstances. Officers who lead soldiers into battle are scared because no matter how experienced they may be, they are facing a new situation and a different task and, thus, the unknown. So is the newly appointed corporate executive or high school principal or college football coach or the physician heading into a surgical suite for the very first time. Each of these people may fear something different, something unique to his situation—fear of failure, fear of personal injury, fear of embarrassment, fear of harming someone else—but they are bound by the thoroughly human experience of being frightened by the prospect of facing the unknown. It is a universal experience.

How does courage under fire relate to leadership? Well, as Rudyard Kipling once wrote, "If you can keep your head when all about you are losing theirs . . . [then] you'll be a Man . . ."* Leadership requires courage—the courage to remain calm and thoughtful and to behave in a manner that inspires others, even when circumstances would be more than enough to cause a breakdown in rational and civilized behavior.

One axiom of leadership is that no one knows everything, and neither do you. It's likely that leaders know more than anyone else

---

*You can access the complete poem "If" by Rudyard Kipling at http://www.online-literature.com/kipling/836.

under their command, but there are plenty of times when information from subordinates is the most critical knowledge that informs decisions. Far more important than fear is your response to it, and it is a healthy thing for any person who aspires to a position of leadership to ask "How do I overcome fear?" The simple answer is "Exercise courage." Distilled to its essence, courage is nothing more or less than a triumph of the human spirit in the face of fear.

COURAGEOUS—OR FOOLISH?

There is no shortage of misguided actions and inappropriate behaviors that are sometimes mistaken for courage. For example, how would you describe a person who is willing to stand up to a herd of charging elephants? Is that courage? Well, I guess it depends on the context, but in most cases I would find that person to be less courageous than merely foolish.

Let's say you happen to stumble upon someone stealing a car. Is it courageous to confront that person, who may or may not be armed, especially if you are unarmed? Or is the more prudent and courageous course of action to call the police? I would argue the latter choice is the better choice unless you saw a life-threatening outcome if some sort of intervention were not immediate. The only option that I would find unacceptable in that scenario would be to turn a blind eye to the entire matter.

What if you happen to come upon an assault being committed, and you decide to dive in at the risk of getting seriously hurt because you believe someone's life is in imminent danger? There is no question that this is a courageous act. But what if you have young children at home who depend on you? Does the benefit in this case outweigh the risks?

As you can see, there is nuance to this discussion. Some acts that are routinely described as courageous are really nothing more than reckless. The thrill seeker is not a hero although, sadly, one is sometimes mistaken for the other. Is wrestling an alligator, chasing tornadoes, or running with bulls an intelligent thing to do? Is that the kind of courage that produces great leadership? I seriously question the wisdom of such behavior—there is, after all, an uninformed aspect to some types of courage that you read about on the obituary pages. People who earn a living doing work that is inherently dangerous—firefighters, police officers, soldiers—understand the difference. There are occasions when these professions require feats of bravery, but the practitioner who hopes to have a long career learns early on that there is a difference between courage and recklessness.

Good leaders take themselves and their training seriously, and they put themselves (and others) at risk only when absolutely necessary. Professionals go about their business with intelligence and thoughtfulness, and that is how leaders behave.

No one wants to work for a boss, or serve under an officer, whose idea of courage is risky, potentially dangerous behavior.

This may sound counterintuitive coming from a lifelong military man, but I believe it's important to exercise care when celebrating courageous behavior. By that I do not mean to imply that courage is a concept unworthy of celebration; nor do I think that anyone who exhibits bravery should be denied recognition for his act. Rather, I simply believe that it's prudent to consider the rationale for an act and to examine closely and carefully whether it was fueled by intelligence and valor, with an eye toward some greater good, or whether it was merely accomplished in the pursuit of a frivolous nature like a thrill. There is a difference, and it's important to be aware of that difference. No one wants to work for a boss or serve under an officer whose idea of courage is risky, potentially dangerous behavior.

Good leaders will exercise courage but will minimize risk at every turn in order to protect those who look to them for guidance. A foolish and reckless leader, on the other hand, will quickly lose the support of subordinates. For them, the instinct for survival will kick in, and the first priority will be to ignore the orders of the leader.

Real courage, however, is a tonic for those who are witnesses or participants in the act. Courage that comes from a place of goodness and benevolence . . . from a place of honesty . . . from the *heart*— that type of courage is stunning, even awe-inspiring. We see examples of it in the Congressional Medal of Honor—some recipients are recognized posthumously; others like Jack Jacobs live through their experiences, and when you read of their heroic deeds, you can't help but wonder, *How were they able to do that?*

Good leaders will exercise courage but will minimize risk at every turn in order to protect those who look to them for guidance.

It goes back to basics: character, training, and the faith a person has in the assigned mission. At some point in the heat of battle, the person stands up and says, "This is what I'm going to do." It comes instinctively from the education, training, and inspirations internalized from past experience.

It sometimes may appear to witnesses as if the courageous are merely taking the dog for a walk when what they are really doing is something so spectacular, so brave that it almost defies comprehension. I know from speaking to some of them that they don't do it with the idea that they're going to lose their lives. Oh, sure, I suppose they figure such an outcome might be possible, and perhaps the image of death, whatever that is, flashes through their minds for an instant . . . but then again, maybe not. Retrospectively, some honorees have said, "Yeah, when that was going on, it did occur to me I might get killed." But I don't think that's what was foremost in their minds. They're simply *reacting* . . . and the nature of that reaction stems from the training they have received, their backgrounds, their emotional makeups, and their faiths. All of these things inform whether people are capable of acting with courage.

A SUBTLER KIND OF COURAGE

When we think of courage, we generally think of an internal response that compels someone to stand up to a threatening situation. More often than not, the threat is of a physical nature. In the everyday world of private business or peacetime in the army, however, it's far more likely that a leader will need to summon courage of another type. This kind of courage is quieter, subtler, but no less important. It's the type of courage that allows you to admit when you're wrong or to make an adjustment in strategy because everyone around you and you yourself realize that something has to change. It's the kind of courage that allows you to give up control and delegate responsibility even though your inclination is to micromanage.

We've all known people who think the boss should work harder than anyone else, and there is some truth to that. The question is, How do you define *hard work*? It's more than just rolling up your sleeves, and it is certainly not about trying to do everyone else's job. It's about putting in the time and creating an atmosphere in which subordinates can thrive and feel good about the work they're doing.

One of the most challenging things for me as a young lieutenant leading my first platoon was to let go of the notion that I had to do everything myself. Sometimes that may indeed be the easiest way to accomplish a task, but it's not always the smartest or most effective path to creating a cohesive unit. It takes courage to assign a task to someone when you aren't sure that person is capable of completing the task or, at least, you're reasonably confident that you could do the job better. It is absolutely an act of courage on the part of a leader to say, "Specialist Jones, this is your responsibility. Do the job," and then stand back and let the Joneses succeed or fail based on their own abilities and ambitions and the training the leader has provided. That takes courage as a leader because there is a very real risk that Jones will fail and the unit will suffer as a result.

Naturally then, there are folks who feel that leadership requires them to do everything for everybody else. That, in essence, degrades leadership. Why? Because first of all, how are the subordinates ever going to learn if they don't get a chance to do the job on their own and make mistakes? And if they don't learn before the real crises arrive, how will they perform when they haven't learned, and there's no one else to do the job for them?

It is absolutely an act of courage on the part of a leader to say, "Specialist Jones, this is your responsibility. Do the job," and then stand back and let the Joneses succeed or fail based on their own abilitties and ambitions and the training the leader has provided.

A powerful element of courage is delegating authority. It may not sound particularly glamorous or courageous, but to me it's a vital part of courageous leadership: letting your subordinates fail, knowing up front that it may well reflect badly on you because your unit didn't measure up when the Joneses faltered.

Don't think that doesn't cross the mind of every young lieutenant when platoon tests are under way! That's why so many leaders refuse to let go of anything. They micromanage not because they love their work or want to make life easier for those in their employ but because they are frightened by the prospect of failure. What these leaders fail to understand is that this reluctance to delegate, in and of itself, represents a fundamental and profound lack of courage . . . a real failure. Teaching, guiding, providing subordinates with the opportunity to succeed on their own—these are all elements of good leadership. And it takes courage to do the job right.

WHEN *NOT* TO DELEGATE

Since life is rarely black and white, and leaders find themselves repeatedly dealing with shades of gray, I should point out here that there are times when leadership demands that one *not* delegate an assignment. The reasons for this are myriad and complicated. There may be safety issues, or there may be morale issues. Undeniably, there are times when a leader can gain credibility and respect by choosing to do something himself, rather than handing the job to a subordinate. If this job requires courage, well, so be it.

I faced precisely this dilemma when I was at Camp Century on the Greenland ice cap, overseeing the shutdown and disassembly of the nuclear power plant that had been installed as the camp's energy source when it was built four years earlier. Our mission was to load the disassembled power plant on specially constructed sleds and ship it back to the coast, from where it would be sent to the National Reactor Test Station in Arco, Idaho.

As the operation progressed and areas surrounding the reactor vessel were exposed, it became clear that the reactor was still producing unanticipated high levels of radiation. The problem was we didn't know precisely how high the levels were or the exact areas where additional shielding would be needed and how much. We had to have answers to these questions in order to complete the shutdown and disassembly of the plant.

The crisis came to our attention at three o'clock in the morning, in the middle of the "graveyard" shift—a macabre note in itself. We were on a tight schedule because the few short months of weather that allowed us to work with the tunnels open were quickly disappearing. So this was a problem that had to be addressed—immediately. Radio communication was all we had, and it was very limited in the Arctic environment. There was no time to call back to the States and wait for technical help; it was up to us. So we reported the situation back to our command group at Fort Belvoir, Virginia, and went at it ourselves.

Rather than assign a possibly life-threatening task to one of my crew members, who were all noncommissioned officers and enlisted men, I decided to go into the reactor tunnel myself to measure the actual radiation levels and try to find the answers. On some level, that was an act of courage. But it was not a reckless or self-aggrandizing act. I knew what I was doing, had weighed the risks and benefits, and determined that it made sense for me, as the commander, to embrace this assignment on my own.

Of course there was risk involved in entering the high radiation areas and taking measurements around the reactor. I wouldn't exactly say it was a foolhardy act for me to assign the task to myself, but there was only one boss, one officer, and that was me. We were in a remote location, and I could not easily be replaced in the event of an injury or illness. But at the same time, I knew that if radiation levels were really excessive, to the point of being potentially deadly, I'd be alerted (by using a portable radiation detector) before I came in close proximity, giving me a window of opportunity during which

I could retreat with relative safety. Radiation exposure is not like getting hit by a bullet; it takes time to do significant damage. Or, at least, I calculated that would be the case.

So I decided to do the job myself because it was the quickest and most efficient path to resolving the problem. No one would have to be briefed, make the surveys, and then piece together a report for me to decide what to do. And quite naturally, I did not feel right assigning the task to anyone else. High radiation is a scary thing. We were not that far removed from the specter of the havoc created by the Hiroshima and Nagasaki atomic bombs, and everyone on the crew had been trained in the effects of radiation exposure.

As it turned out, the radiation levels on the upper deck of the reactor where I took all the measurements topped out at two thousand Roentgens per hour. That's enough to produce a lethal dose in about twenty minutes. I recorded the numbers in approximately forty-five seconds, then beat a hasty retreat. With that information, we were able to figure out how to refill and then reshield the reactor tanks, which would reduce the radiation to levels that would be acceptable for disassembly, repackaging, and shipment to Idaho.

That's part of the principle of courage: inspiring faith in others by demonstrating faith of your own, which often means taking calculated risks.

We had a talented group of soldiers in Greenland, working under difficult conditions. I knew that by accepting the risks associated with measuring the radiation levels, I would send a message to this group. It would show them that I had faith in our mission, and faith in them. And I also knew every one of them would be thinking, *Wow, if the captain is willing to do that, we can sure get the rest of the job done!* That's part of the principle of courage: inspiring faith in others by demonstrating faith of your own, which often means taking calculated risks. There is no army handbook that tells you when you have crossed the line separating courage and recklessness. If you're a good leader, you just . . . know.

Age and experience (or youth and inexperience) sometimes play into the equation. We all feel invulnerable when we're young, and this is perhaps especially true of young men and women at the service academies. West Point attracts people who are eager to test themselves in so many ways. Sometimes, in their eagerness to demonstrate leadership, the fine line between bravery and recklessness is crossed; sometimes the distinction between the two is blurred to such an extent that an officer or cadet is forced to question the very nature of courage. That isn't such a bad thing.

I recall a particular incident when I was in Ranger School. We were training in the swamps of the Florida panhandle, based at the ranger camp on an outlying range of Eglin Air Force Base. As I noted earlier, I went through Ranger School in the wintertime, and the weather that year in both the mountains and the swamps was what we called *ranger weather*: cold, rainy, miserable most every day; rivers and streams ran high, and some of the slack water froze in the swamps. As a result, we frequently found ourselves faced with a difficult body of water to cross.

One night there was an emergency, and our patrol was called back to base. With us on every exercise was a senior officer known as a *lane grader,* whose job it was to grade the Ranger trainees on their performances. Well, on our way back to camp, we had to cross a particular river that had been swollen from the rain. It was so dark we weren't sure just how far across it was at that particular point, but it was clear that the current was so strong that few, if any, of us could simply swim to the other side. Someone with a rope tied around him would have to swim across the river and anchor the rope to a tree so the rest of the patrol could hang on to it and pull themselves across. It was our only way out. I volunteered to swim the rope.

I remember feeling something like fear, but also exhilaration. I tied the rope around my waist, stepped into the river, and began to swim. About three-quarters of the way across, the current caught the rope and began pulling me downstream. And I can remember turning and calling out in the dark: "Let out some more rope!" They did, and I reached the other side safely. As did everyone else.

An experience like that will influence your thoughts and actions for many years after. I don't mean to imply that everyone should go out one night and look for a dangerous river to swim, but there will come a time or more than one time in every young leader's life when the chips are down and someone has to step up to take the risk and do the job. That takes courage. The job and the circumstances will dictate what kind of courage. But courage is the hallmark of a good leader.

Courage involves the mental or moral strength to persevere and withstand danger, to resist opposition or hardship; it implies firmness of mind in the face of danger or extreme difficulty. And it also includes the courage to support unpopular causes. Courage can be displayed in so many ways that it spans the entire spectrum of human behavior.

A soldier who walks point on patrol, or an officer who leads soldiers into battle, must have a fundamental type of courage—the warrior's spirit. But that is only one part of the whole. A strong and successful leader must have the courage to stand up for what is right, to defend those who cannot defend themselves. And perhaps above all, good leaders must have the courage to admit when they are wrong and do what must be done to make things right.

LEADERS ARE ACCOUNTABLE

Leaders must be held accountable for everything that happens under their command. That's one of the first things you're taught at West Point: when you're in charge, you take responsibility. You, as the leader, must have the courage to accept accountability. If things fail to work out as you had hoped, then you must have the courage to step up and say, "Folks, I'm the one who led you wrong. We made a mistake, but I'll make sure we do it right next time." That takes enormous courage because it flies in the face of our natural instincts of self-preservation. Self-preservation isn't merely about staying alive; it's also about saving face. A good leader has to avoid the trap of trying to rationalize poor decisions.

★ ★ ★

That's one of the first things you're taught at West Point: when you're in charge, you take responsibility.

Responsibility and accountability are fundamental to the training a cadet receives at the U.S. Military Academy. We do this by parceling out duty in such a way that even the most mundane of activities carries with it a degree of responsibility. Whatever is happening at the Academy, at any time of the day or night, you can be sure that someone is in charge of that activity. Whether it's intramural sports, distribution of mail, a parade, or simply being the cadet in charge of quarters—everyone has a job. And cadets realize early on that every job is to be done well, and there are consequences to not doing the job well. Of course, no one expects constant perfection. Small transgressions are going to happen all the time—that's part of the learning process—but they aren't overlooked. Cadets are counseled and disciplined for failing to meet their responsibilities, and in that way they not only are taught to distinguish right from wrong in a procedural sense but also, more importantly, come to embrace the notion of accountability.

Over time, these little building blocks of responsibility come together and form a foundation, so when cadets graduate from West Point, they not only know what is expected of them but also feel compelled to perform their duties in a manner consistent with those expectations.

COURAGE INFORMS DECISION MAKING

We have been talking about certain types of behavior that are characteristic of good leadership, and I want to reiterate an important point here: I have gathered these thoughts together under the principle of courage because these are the things that give cadets the strength to make good decisions—even under duress. Think about it: the idea of being responsible and accountable is easily internalized. A cadet thinks, *I'm supposed to march my unit from point A to point B. But then I find out that B has changed. What do I do now? Do I freeze, do I ask for help . . . or do I have the courage to make a decision on my own, to take a different course?* Well-trained leaders will have the courage to make decisions on their own and to live with the consequences of those decisions.

Right or wrong.

5

PERSEVERANCE

There is only one sure way to fail: give up.
—THE AUTHOR

Perform a character assessment of any great leader, and you're bound to discover that he possessed a dogged determination that was essential to his success.

The ability to see things through, to finish what you start, is critical to achieving any goal and not simply because every journey is a series of small steps. Perseverance is an admirable, highly visible trait that fosters confidence in subordinates. There is a dependable nature to it. The old cliché about management by walking around is true: showing up, day after day after day in the most arduous circumstances, really is a big part of the job. "Face time" or "being there" requires perseverance and promotes dependability. Subordinates need to know that the old man is around even when the going is toughest.

One of the most powerful things that occurs at the U.S. Military Academy is young officers taking time to get to know younger cadets who will one day be their subordinates. They'll see each other again downstream—in combat, in the field, at the Pentagon. That sense of being part of something bigger than oneself, again, comes from the leader's perseverance: making the effort to be around for the young folks, and the relationships it fosters with a concomitant sense of shared obligation.

Perseverance is unique in that it is the one common characteristic of all success. Of the principles discussed in this book, perseverance is the only one that is absolutely critical. You might find a successful leader who lacks great courage or vision or faith. (Personally, I think that any leader who has failed to internalize every one of these principles to a significant degree is a flawed leader, but I can't deny that one might find a certain level of success even without possessing these traits in great measure.) But I would be hard-pressed to name anyone who has achieved long-term success in a given field without exhibiting a good deal of perseverance. It simply comes with the territory.

That may not be good news for a society plagued by an ever-shrinking attention span (blame the Internet, blame twenty-four-hour cable television, blame an educational system that measures success by the numbers who are promoted to the next grade level—blame whomever or whatever you like), but it happens to be true. Success is achieved most reliably and efficiently by embracing a willingness to do the work. There is no substitute, no shortcut for good old-fashioned sweat and toil. Good leaders know this, and they demonstrate their willingness to grind it out to everyone under their tutelage. Success ultimately comes from hard work, and the most successful people are usually the ones who are willing to work harder than anyone else—day in and day out.

Perseverance is not only a fundamental building block of success but also one of the most visible principles of leadership. Moreover, it's communicable and contagious: people can pick it up simply by being in close proximity to a strong, determined leader.

That's the beauty of perseverance: it's easily and smoothly transmitted! All you have to do is show up every day and do the best job you are capable of doing. I assure you that the effort will not go unnoticed. But the opposite is true also. Your lack of effort doesn't go unnoticed either. Many, if not most, of us have been in assignments and workplaces in which the boss was the first person out the door each evening. How does that affect morale? How does it impact productivity? Negatively, of course. Just as perseverance is transmitted to the rank and file so, too, are laziness and apathy. Trust me: if the boss doesn't care, then no one will care. If the boss isn't willing to work hard, then no one will work hard. That's not hard to understand. That's just good old human nature and common sense.

By persevering, you are demonstrating strength of character and a desire to lead. People can see that you're the man or woman who is pushing, not giving up, and it communicates to everyone around you that you are taking your work and yourself seriously. It's leading by example, and it is a key principle to the leadership package. You can have all of these other attributes—honor, faith, courage—and yet if you lack perseverance, you are destined to fall short of your goals, whatever they may be. Setbacks come with the territory. Mistakes will be made, tests will be failed, games will be lost, and promotions will be delayed. The point is not necessarily to be the first person across the finish line. The point is to realize that there is no "finish line" in life until the bugler blows taps over your last resting place. Life is a long and demanding race, an ever-expanding and ever-changing series of challenges. If you want to grow as a leader, and as a human being, you keep working at it; you accept the idea that perfection is neither attainable nor desirable. Improvement is the goal. And it never stops moving, so you have to persevere to attain the next level. Over and over, again and again.

★ ★ ★

You can have all of these other attributes—honor, faith, courage—and yet, if you lack perseverance, you are destined to fall short of your goals, whatever they might be.

For a leader, communicating this characteristic (sometimes referred to as *stick-to-it-ivity*) is more a matter of persistence than cleverness. When I decided to write this book, I wanted to talk about the principles that have helped shape my own life as a leader in the military and private sector. More than that, however, I wanted to make it abundantly clear that almost anyone can achieve the success he seeks by becoming a good leader. But you have to understand the simple things that have to be done and want it badly enough to do them. There is work involved, and there is a necessary commitment to the ideals that reflect your leadership to others, but if you want it, you can do it.

THE LASTING VALUE OF "FACE TIME"

The notion of being visible is an integral part of perseverance. As a leader, you want those beneath you to say with confidence and satisfaction, "Hey, I saw the old man the other night. Guess he's keeping an eye on things." The idea is not to convey an atmosphere of suspicion (*Big Brother is watching!*) but rather to project a sense of interest and concern (*We're all in this together!*). There were numerous occasions when I was a battalion commander in Vietnam or a company commander in Germany or the senior officer at Camp Century, Greenland, when just being there was such a big part of the job. I never felt obligated to throw my rank around, to bark out orders, or to micromanage a situation. Beyond handling the myriad organizational and managerial tasks that came with each job, I made it a point to just show up—day or night, weekday or weekend, in places where I was expected and places where I knew I was not expected.

I'd walk around and just chat with the troops and the junior officers. Rarely was there a specific task associated with any of these visits. They merely represented face time and that old cliché again: management by walking around. And I believe in my heart that my commitment to this aspect of the job was every bit as important to my success as an army officer as anything else I might have done.

Get to know the men and women who work for you. They are not just employees or subordinates; they are your lifeblood. They deserve your respect, your attention, and your commitment; and good leadership means you make sure they get all three and that they know they are getting them.

My advice to you, as an upcoming leader, is simply this: get out of the office as often as you can. Open the door, walk around, and shake hands with those whose paychecks you sign. Give them a smile and a friendly greeting. Get to know the men and women who work for you. They are not just employees or subordinates; they are your lifeblood. They deserve your respect, your attention, and your commitment; and good leadership means you make sure they get all three and that they know they are getting them.

So much of life is a matter of showing up. It's not about being flashy or outrageous or calling attention to yourself. In the context of leadership, it's quite the opposite. It's about demonstrating reliability and perseverance, that you care enough to be there so that this type of conversation, in your absence, becomes commonplace:

"Hey, the old man was here again this morning when we were bringing the new recruits in."

"Really, what did he do?"

"Well, he looked around, talked with us for a while, asked Sergeant Jones a few questions, and then he left."

"Yeah? That's nice."

Not exactly dramatic stuff, is it? But it's effective and meaning-ful. (As an aside, *old man* is a term of endearment that you'll find widely used in the military when referring to male superiors. It's even applied to young officers, once they've made an impact and earned the respect of the men and women in their units. The chap-lains usually know who has been awarded the old man sobriquet. Old man is perhaps the only differentiator between men and women that I found in the army when subordinates referred to their supe-riors. Female officers were always referred to by rank and name in my presence.)

This part of perseverance, just being there, is about human interaction and demonstrating a willingness to reach out and be involved in the lives and the work of those with whom you share a mission—without being overbearing or intrusive. Your message is one of trust and confirmation of the good job they are doing, before and after you show up. It connotes a sense of mutual commitment to a shared objective: *we're all here, and we're all going to get the job done together.*

You've probably heard of the phrase I used a couple of times here already: management by walking around (MBWA). I have on occasion heard that acronym used derisively as if little or anything of importance is accomplished. Dead wrong, in my opinion. MBWA is an effective and time-tested managerial strategy that I have employed to great effect throughout my career.

In the dark days of Frequency Electronics, as we attempted to navigate a prosecutorial maze, I learned once again exactly how important it is for a leader to be visible—especially in times of hard-ship or duress. The company, as I wrote in the first part of this book, was devoting an inordinate amount of time to defending itself in court, and there was a distinct possibility that even if found inno-cent of all charges, Frequency Electronics would not have the finan-cial strength to survive the battle. There is nothing quite as damaging to the morale of a workforce as the unknown: Will we still be around next month? Will I have a job? Employees in that scenario face every day with trepidation. They fear for their livelihoods, their families, their reputations.

I couldn't completely eradicate their concerns, but the fact that I showed up each morning and spent a good deal of time walking around and talking to folks sent a message to the workforce. Being there encouraged them to believe that we would not go out of business and that Frequency Electronics would endure and even thrive in the not-too-distant future.

That's perseverance. As a leader, you promote it, you inspire it, and if you're good enough at it, you will foster a real sense of dependability throughout the organization. Others will look at you and think, *If the boss is here, then I'll be here.*

You'll also find that, as a leader, you'll reap great benefits from MBWA. It's a two-way street. By projecting an image of dependability, of perseverance, you cultivate a dependable workforce. Let's face it: the higher you climb in the chain of command—whether you're a general in the army or the CEO of a Fortune 500 company—the more people you have working beneath you, and the harder it is to control everything that happens on your watch. That is the nature of the beast. To succeed as a leader, you must be able to rely on those who work for you, and they're far more likely to be dependable if they know that they, in turn, can depend on you. The balance of power is not equal. You, after all, are the boss, but leadership is a reciprocal arrangement, a two-way street: if you lead, the rest will have to follow, or your leadership will achieve nothing. Any leader would do well to keep that always in mind.

Another interesting side note here: some lecturers on leadership will start their remarks by suggesting that successful leadership requires the boss figure out which way the organization is moving, then run around and get in front of it. That's facetious, of course, but it also reflects some worldly wisdom based on human nature. Sometimes the collective wisdom of subordinates or employees can be one of the most important elements of decision making for the leader. How do you tap into that collective wisdom? MBWA.

When we are all part of the same organization, encouraging dependability promotes unity across the ranks. Never underestimate your reach. The man or woman in charge touches everyone, whether you realize it or not. If you do nothing at all—if you sit cloistered in your office all day and let events wash over you—your very inaction has ramifications, and the chances are you won't like any of them.

> **Here's something you should always remember: if you are the boss, if you are the leader, everything you do sends a signal of one sort or another. You have the ability to control the message.**

Conversely, if you are proactive, forward thinking, and involved—*a real live human with thoughts and foibles you share with peers and subordinates*—that, too, has an effect on the organization. I'm sure I don't have to tell you that the latter approach is far more likely to yield positive results. Perseverance makes this possible. It's not just showing up; it's *when* you show up and the attitude you express when you are visible. Perseverance, like all of the principles of leadership, can and must be communicated to those around you.

It's not uncommon to hear someone suggest, rather matter-of-factly, that leadership requires communication. And it does. Why then is communication not one of the principles of leadership I cite in this book? The answer is simple: communication folds into every one of these principles, since what you are trying to do is communicate with subordinates that you have faith . . . confidence . . . courage . . . perseverance. You're communicating these things all the time through deeds, words, and body language.

Here's something you should always remember: if you are the boss, if you are the leader, everything you do sends a signal of one sort or another. You have the ability to control the message. Do you want to be perceived as having courage and faith? The messages you send in so many ways overtly or sublimely, tell your subordinates who you are, what you expect, and what they should do to respond to your leadership. If you don't send those messages, they'll make up their own . . . of that you can be sure. So would you prefer that they fabricate what they think is your message because they find you arrogant and aloof?

You have the power to convey an image. It's up to you. But it takes perseverance to do that and to make that image stick.

Perseverance, I can assure you, is a hallmark of the cadet experience at West Point. From the first moments as plebes to graduation day, cadets are tested and pushed; more is demanded of them, and they demand more of themselves than they ever thought possible. It isn't supposed to be easy. Nothing worthwhile is achieved without considerable sweat equity, and cadets understand from day one that quitting has consequences far more severe and long-lasting than failing.

We expect mistakes and setbacks; we do not expect the officer-in-training to be perfect, or anything close to it. The West Point experience is all about teaching and learning; it is about growth and maturing. The principles of leadership are not internalized in a single night or even a single year. They are adopted and absorbed over time, slowly and steadily, until the cadet is transformed into an officer . . . into a leader.

Whether one survives the rigors of plebe summer and the sometimes exhausting routine of Academy life is dependent on a number of factors: ambition, intelligence, physical and emotional strength, and maturity. Talent is not at the top of the list of attributes required for success at West Point. All of the innate ability in the world will not help a cadet who lacks the desire or work ethic to endure the eighteen-hour days that are part and parcel of the plebe routine. Each day must be met on its own terms. Place one foot in front of the other until the shock wears off and suddenly what once seemed overwhelming—the long nights of studying, the memorization of rules and regulations, the physical training—now seems . . . manageable. How does this happen?

Through perseverance.

PERSEVERANCE IN THE CLASSROOM

The attrition rate in the first year at the Academy is approximately 10 percent. The majority of those who wash out do so for reasons related to academic failure. The academic program at West Point, particularly in the first year, is indeed rigorous; however, it's not unmanageable for the men and women who are chosen to join the Corps. From their records we know they have the right stuff to succeed. But reality confronts the record when the constellation of forces that a plebe faces—the challenging academic program, leadership training, athletics—takes its toll. Every select class of new cadets is, by its very nature, fiercely driven to succeed. In some cases, the pressure is too much.

When I was a cadet, I was fortunate enough never to have much difficulty with academics. I didn't have to grind too hard to get decent grades, but from my continued close association with the Academy, it's clear that the regimen is far more demanding for the cadets of today. That's why I am so impressed with the perseverance I see at the Academy. From the standpoint of someone who has been a cadet, instructor, coach, commandant, and vice chairman of the board of trustees, I am hugely impressed by the members of today's Corps and how hard all of them work on their academics. The Academy's academic programs consistently rank at the top of the country's best universities. Why is that important? It takes perseverance to make the grade. You can take that to the bank.

Another feature of the Academy today is that cadets receive far more individual attention than their counterparts of fifty years ago. But they face far greater challenges too. Much more is expected of them, and their training is far more detailed and rigorous than it's ever been. The Academy experience teaches youngsters a cold, hard lesson: it isn't possible to have everything at once. As a cadet, you will inevitably find yourself in circumstances in which you can't possibly accomplish everything on your plate; the workload will accumulate to the point where you simply can't get it all done. No amount of effort or scheduling wizardry is going to change that reality. But you don't give up. You set priorities, just as you must as an officer, and you *persevere*. And that part of the game doesn't change when you move into the business world.

Assignments are stacked on top of each other for a reason: to see how cadets can handle pressure. Will they fold? Will they quit? Or will they persevere? In most cases, if the answer is "persevere," the cadet manages to make it through plebe year. In some cases, however, additional measures must be taken: tutoring, receiving extra instruction, repeating a course, and so forth. The Academy excels at this phase of cadet development. After spending enormous resources to recruit and train the cadets, it makes good economic and human capital sense to do all we can to retain those we inducted on the first day of Beast Barracks.

> The Academy experience teaches youngsters a cold, hard lesson: it isn't possible to have everything at once. As a cadet, you will inevitably find yourself in circumstances in which you can't possibly accomplish everything on your plate.

There will be times, however, when those who were selected find the regimen too hard and the experience beyond their capability to endure. Academy life is not for everyone, but for those who truly desire a challenge and who want to embrace the ideals of the army and become leaders, West Point is a magnificent training ground. I believed that when I was a cadet, and my belief was confirmed when I was commandant, and I believe it even more firmly now. And at the end of the day, the most important thing for every cadet is to be able to look in the mirror and say, "I did all I could, the best I could."

And at the end of a rigorous four-year academic and military program, about 80 percent of the original plebe class will walk up to the graduation dais and be awarded their diplomas and gold second lieutenants' bars. While there is a perception that most cadets who withdraw or otherwise fail to thrive at a service academy do so largely because of the physical demands of Academy life, this is not the case at West Point. Most cadets find the academic component to be by far the most challenging aspect of their education, and this is the cause of most separations both during and after plebe year.

PERSEVERANCE ON THE ATHLETIC FIELD

When General Douglas MacArthur became superintendent of the Academy in 1919, he instituted the cadet intramural athletic program, the most extensive intramural program of all colleges in the country. Since athletic participation is a great teacher of perseverance for young men and women, it should come as no surprise that it is now mandatory at West Point (either at the intramural or intercollegiate level). By and large, though, the young men and women who enter West Point have a history of athletic accomplishment; physical fitness is already an important part of their lives.

There is, however, a significant difference between intramural and intercollegiate athletics. The latter is highly demanding. The Academy competes at the Division I level in all major sports, and thus, participation in varsity sports requires a huge commitment in time and energy from cadets who are involved at this level. This serves to intensify the demands of the academic experience as well, for the cadet student-athletes often find themselves with an open book propped on their lap, barely able to keep their eyes open, while riding home from an away game late at night.

But I must say from long experience at West Point that rigorous time demands do not dissuade many cadets from competing on varsity teams, teams that are very competitive on the national level. Playing on a varsity team is an important goal for a very significant number of cadets, many of whom have been at least partially defined by their accomplishments on the playing field. My experience in teaching, coaching, and commanding the Corps of Cadets has firmly convinced me that cadets are more capable than any of their peers at other institutions when it comes to melding sports and academics at the collegiate level. Certainly, it makes sense at West Point, where so many of the lessons learned in athletic competition—teamwork, discipline, confidence—are transferable to the military in general and the battlefield in particular.

I'm going to blow my own horn here and tell you a little bit about my athletic career at West Point because it has everything to do with perseverance. (Granted, this is not an example of persevering as a leader but rather persevering as a person.) Football was an important part of my experience during my four years as a cadet.

I considered it a huge personal challenge to make the varsity team because I was not (and still am not today) a big man.

So how did I earn a varsity letter on one of the strongest college football teams in the country at the time? Four words: *I just kept going.* Some folks quit; some settled for being practice players; and others got hurt. I got hurt too—that comes with the territory in college football. But I just kept going. I came back from a disabling knee injury and essentially started over again to work my way back up. I showed up for practice and gave my best effort every day.

There was no doubt among the coaches or my teammates—many of whom were bigger, stronger, faster, and more gifted athletes than I was—that I wanted to be part of that football team. In my mind, I had decided that nothing short of a career-ending injury would prevent me from playing. Believe me—I was not a great football player, but there I was, playing, and playing a lot, because in those days teams were allowed only two substitutions per quarter, and everybody played both offense and defense.

How did I earn a varsity letter on one of the strongest college football teams in the country at the time? Four words: *I just kept going.*

It led to Army's coach, Colonel Red Blaik, naming me a field captain and, I'm sure, to people looking at me in a different light, perhaps thinking, *Hmm . . . you were a varsity football player at West Point; you played under Red Blaik when Vince Lombardi was one of his top assistants. Well, you must have something going for you if you did that.*

Making the football team, against fairly steep odds, gave me enormous confidence in other areas of my life. It happened not because of God-given talent but primarily because I was willing to stick to it and work at it to the best of my ability and admittedly limited skills. I persevered . . . and that perseverance paid off. That's why I can stand up and say with assurance that perseverance is such an important building block in the construction of good leaders.

Simply put: good leaders don't quit, and that point is made clear to cadets at West Point from the moment they arrive on the Academy grounds. It is understood that there will be mistakes; working with human beings is an imprecise exercise, and no one expects perfection. The idea is to keep moving—to *persevere*.

The lessons I learned at West Point served me well throughout my career in the army as well as in private industry and the nonprofit world. More examples come to mind, which I cite mainly to show how they relate to the principles of leadership that matter most to young and old alike.

I look back with great appreciation on my experiences as a junior officer in the occupation army after World War II in Germany. I was a company commander when we went on bridge-building exercises across various bodies of water—the Rhine, Neckar, and Danube rivers among them. At times we encountered weather and terrain conditions that made it virtually impossible to get where we wanted to go and do what we were assigned to do. That doesn't mean we quit; we did everything humanly possible to accomplish our assigned missions, but in the end, nature sometimes proved to be too much for us.

★ ★ ★

You will come up against obstacles that can be neither surmounted nor removed. But never do you come away from such an experience without learning and growing as a leader.

We knew beforehand that "a bridge too far" was often purposely assigned in order to test the unit when it encountered uncharted waters. We were evaluated on these exercises, and our scores reflected not merely whether the task was completed but how we handled adversity and disappointment. So we went through circumstances where no matter how hard we tried, we just couldn't make it work.

Training and experience, however, have taught me that there are numerous ways to measure success. Failing to complete these exercises did not ever cause me to think that perseverance doesn't work. You should keep in mind that some tasks are impossible, and there are going to be times when you, as a leader, will come up against obstacles that can be neither surmounted nor removed. But never do you come away from such an experience without learning and growing as a leader.

In circumstances such as these, when do you make the decision to throw in the towel? Typically, in the military, that happens somewhere up the chain of command, and it happens quite naturally, when everyone comes to the realization that folks at the bottom—the troops on the ground—are just not going to be able to get the job done, despite their best efforts. There is, then, a limit to what perseverance can achieve. We can say in idealistic terms that perseverance is like a ram butting a dam: he doesn't stop until either he or the dam breaks. In point of fact, however, there are limits to what perseverance can achieve, and it's important for leaders to recognize these limits. Perseverance is not synonymous with stubbornness (although it's fair to say that most people who do not give up easily have a deep stubborn streak!); it's more subtle than that. Ideally, perseverance is informed action, and it's exercised with judgment and intelligence.

A key aspect of each of the principles that I am laying out in this book is that they appeal to a leader's sense of community: we are part of something bigger. I believe the highest calling for which we are put on this earth is to serve our fellow man, and I'm convinced that really successful leaders have to think that way. Being an effective leader is not about personal glory; it's about recognizing that we are all pieces of the puzzle, and trying, to the best of our ability, to fit those pieces together the best way we can in order to get the job done. Perseverance is crucial to the survival and success of any community, and that's why it's such an important principle of leadership.

Within any organization, there will be jobs that are extraordinarily difficult to accomplish, and there will come a time when people will naturally question the viability of the mission: "It's cold, dark, and dangerous. What are we doing here, and why are we doing it?" Faith will sustain us to a point and give us the confidence that everything will turn out all right. But it's not going to turn out all right if we quit. That's why perseverance is so important: without it, there is literally no chance for success. After all, you can't succeed if you quit or don't even try. Nothing that's worth achieving is done without great effort; and great effort, by its very nature, is going to require perseverance. It's a fact of life.

I believe the highest calling for which we are put on this earth is to serve our fellow man, and I'm convinced that really successful leaders have to think that way.

PERSEVERANCE IN THE BUSINESS WORLD

Perseverance is no less important to the business world, which may, at least partially, account for the large number of West Point graduates who have carved out extremely successful careers in the private sector after they've left the military. What I could call *corporate perseverance* is just as important to the success of any company as it is to individuals. And obviously, one way to encourage perseverance in business (and this is an option unavailable in the military) is to offer financial incentive. There's nothing wrong with this. Indeed, if financial compensation is a tool at your disposal, then you would be limiting yourself by not including it in your inventory of rewards for performance. The employee who works hardest and longest deserves recognition—and that means more than just a pat on the back or a nod from the boss.

But if you're running a business, you can't use compensation indiscriminately because resources are not unlimited. So there's a judicious application of the kinds of incentives that can encourage people to see that persevering is the right thing. (A note of caution is appropriate here: the most important features of any incentive compensation program are fairness and repeatability. Much harm can be done with poorly planned or indiscriminate compensation packages.)

A leader in the private sector must rely on instinct as well as business acumen to know when perseverance is no longer enough. In other words, a leader knows when to pull the plug. If you can look at your company each day and say to yourself, in all honesty, "We've had failures, things that have sidetracked us, but I think it's going to work out in the end," then perseverance is advised.

That's the way it was for me at Frequency Electronics. I never lost confidence that we would eventually come out of that court case intact. I knew in my heart that nothing had been done wrong— no laws broken, no ethical lines crossed. Moreover, there were clear signals from our customers that our products, both legacy (our current ones) and the new ones we were developing, were going to enjoy increased demand from a growing customer base. That was crucial to my initial involvement and continued perseverance. I had to believe that everyone working with me was being straight with me. And I had to believe that our workforce—our top engineers and scientists and skilled, highly experienced laborers—would be able to develop and build the products that would bring us back into the highly competitive marketplace. I had also done my homework—I had documented evidence that helped me make an informed decision.

Nevertheless, we were getting hammered every day; our resources were being siphoned off, and employees—good people—were jumping ship. It took more than a modicum of perseverance for me (and others) to forge ahead. As I wrote earlier, after a long, arduous legal odyssey, Frequency Electronics survived and has prospered very handsomely in the years since. Certainly, a lot of good work was done by many good people who shared that perseverance and helped us through a long, dark night. I don't think there's anything I could have accomplished in the private sector that gives me a greater sense of satisfaction and quiet pride.

We persevered—and without the training I had received at West Point and in the military, it's pretty clear to me that I would not have had the strength to see it through.

6

CONFIDENCE

I'm sure this will work if I can find a bigger hammer.
—ANONYMOUS

There are three types of confidence essential to leadership. One is the confidence required to give advice and to dispense orders, even when faced with unknowns and the unknowable. The second is being confident and comfortable enough with yourself that you can ask for advice from others. And third is the confidence to depend on subordinates, to delegate authority and stand back to let them do the job. Don't ever overlook number three. It's critical that you have enough confidence in subordinates to give them opportunities to succeed, and to fail.

For even the most gifted leaders, this can be a deceptively challenging concept to grasp. We talk about it a lot at West Point: how the Academy wants to build military leaders who will let their subordinates fail. Why is this so critical? We spend most of our lives in the army preparing for war; if you don't have the opportunity to fail and learn from your mistakes during preparation, then you're at great risk of finding yourself incapacitated when the stakes are much higher, when the harsh conditions of real war come along.

Let's be clear on one thing here: I'm talking about the everyday life of soldiers, training for combat that may never occur. But this also includes the day-to-day jobs that we're called upon to perform, some of which are going to have a more serious impact than others. And the most important concept embedded in all of this is trust. As you show confidence in your subordinates, they are going to gain a growing sense that you trust them to do their jobs. This inspires the reciprocal sense that builds their trust in you. A sense of mutual trust between superior and subordinate is one of the most important elements of successful leadership, and it springs from the confidence you demonstrate every day in yourself and, by judicious delegation and mentoring, the confidence you demonstrate in your subordinates.

One of my earliest examples of exposure to this philosophy occurred when I was a junior officer, just a lieutenant, stationed in Germany. I was a combat engineer platoon leader; my noncommissioned officers were all veterans of the Korean War, and some were World War II vets as well. Our critical wartime mission was the emplacement of floating bridges across major rivers in Germany, something I mentioned in the last chapter. We exercised our bridge-building equipment and capabilities every month by executing major river crossings. These included building the standard floating bridges that were part of our army engineer inventory, utilized by the U.S. Army everywhere to get from one side of the water to the other.

There were already permanent bridges in place across the Rhine, but peacetime training requires the execution of contingency plans. In the event that hostilities broke out and major bridges were destroyed or rendered impassable, we had to make sure that our river-crossing capabilities were maintained and temporary bridges could be emplaced to handle the added traffic to and from the front. In this case, the front was the border of East Germany, and our enemy was the massive army of the Soviet Union.

Lieutenants and noncommissioned officers became experts at these operations through regular training in the classroom and out on the rivers of West Germany. The most important river we worked on was the Rhine, which—in its upper reaches between Heidelberg and Karlsruhe—was a fast-flowing, dangerous stretch of water with major industrial traffic, the downstream ships passing at really high speeds. On one of these regular field exercises, everything was going as well as could be expected until my platoon came face-to-face with a nearly catastrophic accident. I was not physically present when the accident occurred, so I was not directly supervising the ongoing work of the troops. Nevertheless, it was my platoon and clearly my responsibility. When I returned to the river after a brief reconnaissance, I found myself confronted with what any new lieutenant would consider a heart-stopping sight. One of our truck-mounted crane operators had lost control of his equipment, and the crane—a massive vehicle with a fifty-foot boom—had somehow slid down a ramp and found its way into the Rhine River!

Fortunately, no one was seriously injured, but there was substantial monetary cost associated with something like this. Even back in the fifties, when war and national security were at the forefront of everyone's concerns, spending money was not done in a cavalier way. Certainly, no young officer wanted to be responsible for an accident of this magnitude; it wasn't exactly the sort of thing that would cast a new, untested young officer in a flattering light.

I can still recall seeing the crane submerged in the Rhine, its boom rising in a sort of comic majesty out of the murky water that was flowing past at high velocity, making a "rooster tail" at the downstream end of the boom. Time and distance have added a little humor to the image, but it was painful to see it when I arrived on the scene moments after it had happened.

My first response, naturally, was to make sure that no one was lost or hurt. My next move was to try to figure out what had happened. I was still in the midst of step two when my commanding officer came along and joined us on the riverbank. This was Captain Ed Scharff—whom I saluted earlier in the book—an enormously thoughtful and intelligent man, a graceful and charismatic leader who inspired confidence in just about everyone in his command—including me. He was the type of CO who delegated comfortably and confidently, presenting opportunities for advancement and creativity to virtually anyone who showed promise.

So you can see right off where I began to learn some of the principles of good leadership. It's a simple formula: express confidence in those you lead, and you instill self-confidence within them. Then, if everything works as it should, they in turn demonstrate confidence to those beneath them. Confidence, when exercised appropriately and regularly, trickles down. And like so many of the principles we're discussing, you don't have to be a rocket scientist to add it to your leadership arsenal.

So there we were, on the banks of the Rhine, our hapless and submerged crane just a few feet away attracting a crowd. Mature and rational leader that he was, Captain Scharff did not rant and rave. He neither chewed me out nor feigned indifference. Rather, he quietly and matter-of-factly asked, "What happened?"

The awkward moment between his question and my answer represented a pivotal point in my professional and personal development, for it posed an ethical quandary. Truthfully speaking, I had nothing to do with the accident. I wasn't actually there when it happened, although I was close by and, by orders, the officer in charge. The operator of the crane had made a mistake while under the direct supervision of one of our sergeants. I was a brand-new junior officer, a fresh-faced raw lieutenant trying to do a good job while earning the respect of my troops and the approval of my superior officers. And now, here I was, trying to explain how this very serious and expensive accident had occurred.

What person in that situation wouldn't be tempted to pass the buck? I don't mean that in the most crass and self-serving way; I simply mean that I had two choices: 1) tell the truth, including the fact that I wasn't there when the crane spilled into the river (thereby implying that I was not responsible for the accident); or 2) accept responsibility, and go from there.

I chose number two.

It wasn't because I felt any attraction to martyrdom or because I wanted to make some sort of bold statement. It just seemed like the right thing to do. More importantly, though, I felt reasonably secure that this accident would not end up with some sort of seismic, career-ending result for me. And the reason I felt this way was because my commanding officer had instilled within me a sense of confidence; I believed that I could tell him what had happened—that I was not on site when the accident transpired—and his response would have been measured and appropriate. I would have been off the hook, but I felt pretty sure that Captain Scharff might have lost some respect for me if I said something to the effect of "I wasn't there; don't blame me!" I know that feeling came from those years at West Point, learning to take responsibility without offering excuses, and it made me feel in my heart—and in my gut—that I could assume responsibility for the accident because it was the right thing to do.

So I told what could technically be called *a little white lie*.

"Captain," I said, "this is my fault. We were off-loading the bridge with this crane, and as I was directing it, whether it was something I didn't make clear or whatever, I don't really know, we lost control, and it went into the river and . . . well, there it is, sir."

The captain nodded.

"So you were here, Lieutenant . . . on site?"

"Yes, sir."

You will make mistakes, as will those who turn to you for leadership and guidance. The point is to persevere and to do so with confidence in your own abilities and in the abilities of those around you.

With those two words—*Yes, sir*—I became officially account-able for the submerged crane and the expense associated with retrieving and replacing it. This represented more than just a meta-phorical stepping up to the plate; it was a public acknowledgment that I had not entirely met the standards and expectations of the job and the rank. In summary, I had failed.

As noted on several occasions in this book, however, failure need not be fatal. As a leader you will surely encounter obstacles that can't immediately be avoided or cleared. You will make mistakes, as will those who turn to you for leadership and guidance. The point is to persevere and to do so with confidence in your own abilities and in the abilities of those around you.

This accident went on my record, and had my CO simply taken the easy path of blaming me and leaving it to a higher authority to mete out the punishment, it could have represented a significant blot. Instead, he reported the accident and assigned no fault to any individual. Did he know, intuitively, what had hap-pened? Or did his first sergeant tell him privately what he learned through the grapevine? Whatever the case, that act by my com-manding officer demonstrated that he had confidence in me. That's the kind of leadership that passes on to subordinates the faith, courage, and confidence to take responsibility. That's what builds good leadership. I learned that from personal experience under a good leader.

I don't mean to imply that I wasn't concerned about the out-come, or even tempted, however briefly, to take the easy way out. As I spoke with Captain Scharff, I can remember thinking to myself, *I know this is the right thing to do,* but it's only human to think a bit about self-preservation in these instances, as well. Therefore, unpleas-ant little thoughts intrude: *Hey . . . wait a minute! Why not dump it on the crane operator? Or the sergeant? You weren't even here! Why should you take the blame?*

> ★ ★ ★
>
> **Three simple words:** *take the blame.*

But that would have been taking the easier wrong; it also would have been an example of failing to exercise courage. In each of the personal experiences I relate here, and many more that I can recall, the principles of leadership are constantly overlapping and intersecting. Simply by actively demonstrating one of them, you find that you are also demonstrating several. Confidence in my superior officer, as well as confidence in my own abilities, gave me the courage to accept responsibility for the accident. The natural and not unpleasant side effect of this action was that it instilled enormous faith (another principle) among my subordinates, who suddenly realized that their new young lieutenant was not afraid to step up and say, "I'll take the blame for this."

It could have backfired, but I felt in my heart that I had handled the situation in an appropriate manner. And while I am now (and certainly was then) a rather guileless fellow, I did recognize that I had been presented with an opportunity to display a fundamental type of leadership: if I wanted to become a leader, the buck, which does indeed stop somewhere, would stop with me.

Three simple words: *take the blame.*

It's not always easy, and it does sometimes carry a risk; however, if you want to be a genuine leader—as opposed to someone who is primarily concerned with rank, advancement, and salary (in other words, *appearances*)—then you must embrace the noble concept of taking responsibility.

Confidence factors into the equation in a couple of ways. First, you need confidence in order to believe that you can survive the fallout that comes with admitting a mistake. Second—and this is perhaps the most important thing—you will gain confidence (and respect) through the act of accepting blame. I'm not talking about incompetence. There is a great difference between someone who repeatedly fails to get the job done in an acceptable manner and someone who is very good at his job yet occasionally makes a mistake. Leaders who are diligent and responsible have the confidence to acknowledge missteps—both their own and those that occur under their command—and to learn from their mistakes. Few things will breed contempt from superiors and dissension among subordinates quite so quickly as a leader who repeatedly screws up and then blames everyone else for his shortcomings.

Few things will breed contempt from superiors and dissension among subordinates quite so quickly as a leader who repeatedly screws up and then blames everyone else for his or her shortcomings.

Not long after the crane did its impersonation of a submarine, an interesting thing happened to me: I was selected for company command, and everyone from the battalion chaplain on down made sure that the troops called me the *old man*. That might not sound significant, but it actually was. If I wasn't the youngest man in the company, I was pretty close to it, and yet I was the company commander. The other leaders in the company and in our battalion went out of their way to make sure that I was accorded the respect (and even affection) typically accorded a company commander, thus their very public use of the term *old man*. It was partially good-humored, but it also made the point. So that's what I was: an old man in his early twenties. And I felt pretty good about it.

CONFIDENCE AND COURAGE

It is important to understand that there are fundamental differences between confidence and courage. They are linked at an elemental level, and each is an essential component of strong leadership.

When I was a battalion commander in Vietnam, I detached a reinforced company from my battalion to support the Fourth Infantry Division during the invasion of Cambodia. Our area of operations, stretching west from the Central Highlands of South Vietnam, was, at the time, an extremely hostile and dangerous place for our army. The Viet Cong had a lot of pretty effective anti-aircraft artillery, and our helicopters were not always surviving very well in that environment.

Because some of my troops were stationed there, I wanted to be sure they were okay, and that meant seeing them personally and letting them see me. This was not something a battalion commander typically did when his troops were attached to another battalion, and certainly it was not something that was expected of me with troops engaged in combat in another country. So the first thing I did was to make sure that my pilots were comfortable with the situation—from the cover they would receive from troops on the ground to the suitability of landing zones. Helicopter pilots in Vietnam had an extraordinarily difficult and harrowing job, and I always sought to let them know that I not only was concerned for their safety but also appreciated their effort and courage. More to the point, when they were flying me around the area of operations, they had to know that the old man was taking the same risks he asked of them. And in the back of their minds they would be telling themselves: *After all, the CO wouldn't risk his life if he didn't have to, would he?*

We filed our flight plans and flew from South Vietnam just a short way into Cambodia and landed at a couple of sites, just to make sure the troops were okay and knew that I was there. Even though most of them were attached to a different unit, I wanted to check on their equipment, ammo, and chow and see if there were any special supplies needed by the combat engineers. In reality, there wasn't much I could do for them, other than make sure they had the resources necessary to accomplish their mission; however, by making the effort and taking the risk to fly in myself, I was telling the troops that their commanding officer was looking out for them.

It's hard to overstate the importance of something like that in a military context, where life and limb are being risked on a daily basis. Soldiers fight; superior officers give the orders and provide the materials for the soldiers to be successful in that fight. In every instance, whether peacetime exercises or wartime operations, it's imperative that the soldiers know that there is legitimate concern for their well-being.

A real possibility existed that my helicopter might have been fired upon and shot down, in which case my decision might have been viewed as lacking discretion. But to me it was important, so I weighed that against the risk. A certain type of courage was involved in that decision—physical courage . . . visceral courage. With this type of courage, one knows there is the possibility that something bad might happen; the result could even be fatal. I accepted that possibility, as did the pilots who agreed to fly me in. I did it for the troops, and the pilots did it for me.

Exercising courage when you know there is danger is part of leadership. Having the confidence to do that—confidence in yourself and the people you depend upon to do that with you—is an essential principle of good leadership, and the leader's display of confidence builds that same sense of confidence in subordinates. It flows both ways.

Confidence also played a role in this decision to the extent that

I had enormous confidence in the abilities of our pilots, and confidence in our troops on the ground. Certainly, I had to call on my courage to order my pilots to fly me into Cambodia, but I felt it was a necessary statement to make, for the troops I had dispatched were facing even greater dangers every waking hour.

Confidence as a separate principle is more nuanced, stemming as it does from experience: you know from practice that what you are going to attempt to do is likely to work. Do not mistake confidence for uninformed bravado. Now, it may well be true that there is an element of uncertainty involved, something that prompts doubt. Confidence will sustain you in these times, permitting you to overcome self-doubt.

It isn't enough, however, for a leader to feel confident about a venture; he or she must be able to transmit that confidence to subordinates. You can't possibly transmit confidence if you have no confidence in yourself. That is something that simply cannot be faked. People will see right through you and immediately lose confidence in you and in the mission.

There are many factors that contribute to the building of confidence, most notably experience and preparation. In every walk of life you're going to encounter things you haven't seen or done before. And that's where having tested yourself earlier, many times, in a variety of challenging experiences that we call training, will give you the confidence to depend on yourself when the chips are down. It's the leader's genuine, built-from-experience confidence that is so important—because that's what inspires others to follow when the situation calls upon everyone to venture into unknown territory.

Building confidence through experience is a hallmark of West Point training. As I wrote in an earlier chapter, cadets are given leadership responsibilities almost from the first day and are assigned a myriad of duties—some mastered with relative ease, others requiring real struggle and, at times, seemingly impossible to master.

Through courage and perseverance, though, the cadets strive on, and in so doing, they accumulate the confidence required to lead others. If you say to people, "This is where we're going," you have to be able to project your confidence that they can do it, and even more important, that it's the right thing to do. This comes through practice and experience—through repeated successes achieved and failures overcome. Again, I want to mark this point well; the principles of leadership are a mosaic, working together to form the whole.

Another way to look at these intersecting, self-reinforcing principles is to consider confidence as something that's external, while courage is internal. So you're demonstrating the principle of confidence by saying, "I'm confident that you can do this job," which helps other folks have confidence in themselves. Confidence from a leader truly inspires performance from others. That's a tremendously important component of leadership, and one that is often overlooked. Think about the boss who browbeats and criticizes, while virtually never handing out a compliment or a word of encouragement. Confidence is positive reinforcement; it's a perfectly human way to approach leadership, and subordinates will respond to it in wholly positive ways.

LEARNING FROM FAILURE

There will be failures and setbacks—that goes without saying. But failure can be a wise and forgiving teacher. We learn from our mistakes, accept responsibility for them, and move on. Handled thoughtfully and positively, failure can actually have the effect of fueling confidence. That's why it's so important for leaders to delegate authority: so that subordinates are given opportunities. Whether these opportunities result in failure or success is almost irrelevant. Far more important is whether one embraces the opportunity, and how one responds to the outcome (success or failure).

Training, which offers the opportunity to fail without consequence, is what builds confidence and prepares the leaders of tomorrow. Nothing feeds confidence quite like preparation. Put another way, there is no substitute for hard work. Courage is important. So are experience and perseverance. But it's clear that you can equate the degree of confidence you have in something with the degree of preparation that you put into it. They go hand in hand. If you're on a job, you have a mission, and you have some experience with it, that obviously helps your confidence. What many people don't take into account, however, is the importance of preparation. Just because you've done something before doesn't mean you no longer have to prepare. The job still requires your attention.

Training, which offers the opportunity to fail without consequence, is what builds confidence and prepares the leaders of tomorrow. Nothing feeds confidence quite like preparation.

Without preparation, there is no real confidence; there is only false bravado.

7

APPROACHABILITY

You catch a lot more flies with honey than with vinegar.
—Old folk saying

History is replete with iconic examples of leadership, one of the most common being the omnipotent leader who stands above all others, casting down wisdom from on high. In my experience, however, an effective leader is someone who can talk with subordinates, and to whom subordinates can talk. In other words, a good leader is approachable.

Let's take a moment to examine this word: *approachability.* *Approach* means to go closer, and *approachable* describes someone who can be approached. So we can take *approachability* to mean the ability of certain people to get other people to approach and talk with them, what I would call a knack for mixing with others on the human level. Taken in the context of leadership, I am talking about leaders who work at setting up situations and an environment in which subordinates feel comfortable, even urged, to approach and, specifically, to communicate with their leaders.

If any organization, military or civilian, is to work well, then subordinates have to feel that they can ask their leaders for guidance and help; they have to feel that they can admit they made a mistake.

The stereotypical military leader is unapproachable, and unfortunately, it's sometimes an accurate stereotype. If you want to guarantee failure, then create an atmosphere in which subordinates are reluctant to share their feelings with you. If any organization, military or civilian, is to work well, then subordinates have to feel that they can ask their leaders for guidance and help; they have to feel that they can admit they made a mistake. If they trust and respect their leaders and know they can approach them when they really feel the need, they'll be far better at their jobs and far more likely to accept order and discipline.

I always cite language as a key measure of approachability. Younger people look to their leaders for guidance: how they walk and talk and otherwise behave. I always remind junior officers that their subordinates really want to imitate their leaders; they don't want their leaders to imitate them. When you sit down and think about that, it tells you pretty clearly that subordinates don't want to hear their leaders using profanity; they know there are better ways to express thoughts, and they want to hear that from their leaders. Deep down inside, they want their leader to set the right example. Or look at it this way: if your subordinates don't care how you talk and behave, it's safe to assume that they really don't care that much for what you might be trying to say or show to them. That's a proven formula for failed leadership. Subordinates want to look up to their leaders.

I'll give you an example. When I was a brigadier general, serving as the assistant commander of the Twenty-fifth Infantry Division in Hawaii, I witnessed a platoon leader working with a group of about a dozen senior noncommissioned officers on a rifle range. He stood in front of the men, critiquing and instructing, and his speech was just filled with expletives. He was a young officer, trying to make a point, and I couldn't help but think that this was precisely the wrong way to foster approachability. He wasn't screaming at them or chastising them; what he was doing was worse. The young officer was laboring under the erroneous assumption that this profane tirade would somehow endear him to the rank-and-file troops: *This is how the soldiers talk; so I'll talk the same way. They'll pass it on, and everyone will know I'm one of the troops.*

Now, it wasn't natural for that youngster to talk like that, and you could tell it from the somewhat stilted nature of his speech. He was not a West Pointer, but he was a commissioned officer. He didn't come from an uneducated or unsophisticated upbringing; he had gone to college. I had seen him behave as an accomplished, erudite young gentleman, more than capable of speaking in thoughtful, normal terms. But here he was, standing up in front of a bunch of troops, thinking this was how he needed to speak and what they wanted to hear. He was clumsy, he was out of character, and he was dead wrong. It gave me a wonderful opportunity—which sticks in my mind very clearly to this day—to approach him afterward, and to let him know, quietly and privately, that he'd demeaned himself with this behavior.

"Lieutenant," I said, "you know, the young men and women in your organization, they really don't want you to be like them; they want to be like you. That's what leadership is all about. Everybody in here should want to be like you, and I don't think any of them would want you to use that kind of language."

The young man was embarrassed. On some level he knew that he had made a poor decision; he just needed to hear it from someone else. But my role in that exchange was important, for it takes us back to approachability. When you give a lecture like that, it can't be delivered in a threatening, disdainful manner. The young officer should come away with his dignity and pride intact, feeling that even though he has been criticized, he understands that you are looking out for him, and his questions and concerns are always welcome. You don't just reprimand and walk away—not if you're trying to help someone become a good leader. The last thing I wanted was for that lieutenant to think, *I'll never talk to that general again!* I wanted him to appreciate the advice I was offering because it was, in fact, good advice that I knew would help him, and I figured he'd ask my advice more than once before our tours with the Twenty-fifth Division were over (which he did).

YOU'RE A LEADER, NOT A PAL

A common mistake for an aspiring leader is to confuse approachability with commonality. To keep this in a military frame of reference, the troops should not look at their superior officers as their pals. They should look at them as their leaders. And what are the things that distinguish you as a leader? What are your standards of behavior? That's where you put this principle of approachability into practice. In all my years in the army, I wanted the troops who were serving under me to know that they could come to me when they had a problem even if they thought it might be pretty far-fetched for me to be able to help them. There were, of course, established parameters. Their leaders also worked for me, and we had a chain of command that was the norm for solving the kinds of problems soldiers (and NCOs) can run into. Soldiers would never approach me to ask if they could borrow ten dollars or to plead for a three-day pass just because they were tired. But if they had serious concerns or if they simply wanted to share whatever was on their minds when our paths crossed, then my office door, so to speak, was always open.

There are times when hairs are split, when a subordinate truly feels that someone in his chain of command has wronged him. So he sidles up to the assistant division commander in the motor pool or out on the rifle range or out at physical training, and he says something like, "Sir, you know my wife is pregnant, and I wanted to spend some more time with her before we deploy to the Big

Island, but my request has been denied. Can you help me?" All of a sudden you're in a situation where the chain of command is being bridged by this huge jump. The young soldier has made a decision to bypass his NCOs and officers, who may have said, "Sorry, we move out Monday, and we need everyone on duty for equipment prep and loading." The young man, however, feels that you, the ADC with the winning smile and affable personality, are so approachable that he can go directly to you and ask you to over-rule the decision.

What do you do in that circumstance? Do you talk to his platoon leader? If so, what do you say to him? And is that the right thing to do anyway?

One option would be to just grab one of the junior officers and say, "What's going on with this soldier? Why can't he have his pass?" That would accomplish two objectives, both of them very negative and counterproductive: it would get the young soldier in a scrape for going over his immediate supervisors to ask for something they had told him he could not have, and it would seriously jeopardize the idea that anyone could talk with the general and know his privacy would be respected.

Or you could say something like this: "Son, I'm not sure what happened here, but I know your lieutenant. And he's a good man—I'm sure of that. He wouldn't be a commissioned officer in this division if he wasn't. You know that too. You're a member of this division, and I know that you're proud of every one of us here. I'm really sorry that something you needed or wanted couldn't get done, but I'll tell you this—I'm sure the right things are going to happen for you. I'm glad you spoke to me, and I hope you will always feel like you can come to your NCOs and officers, and even me if you just want to get something like this off your chest."

You could also follow up on the second option by talking to that young soldier's NCOs and officers, ask them how his wife was doing with her pregnancy, and send them the message that you cared about their soldiers and their weekend operation and understood how it affected all of them. They would get the message.

IT WORKS BOTH WAYS

Approachability, like so many of the leadership principles we're discussing, is a two-way street. You have to handle these sorts of issues with a lot of circumspection, no question about it. But that's one of the biggest challenges of leadership—working around the margins, assessing a situation, and figuring out how to handle it. We lead *people,* and people will always have something going on that challenges your leadership skills in ways you never imagined when you try to help them.

Approachability also refers to a leader's sense of place within an organization. Confident, strong leaders understand their roles and try to establish avenues of approachability, whereby everyone within the organization—above and below—is encouraged to make contact. It fosters a sense of community and demonstrates that the leaders are not above the rules; they're not untouchable. They are part of the organization, and everybody should have the opportunity to feel that they are connected to their leaders not only through the chain of command but also in a more informal way.

We lead *people,* and people will always have something going on that challenges your leadership skills in ways you never imagined when you try to help them.

In today's army, there are so many opportunities for senior officers to spend time with junior officers, and for junior officers to spend time with enlisted men, that it's really inexcusable for a leader to become cloistered or unapproachable. When a leader is approachable, subordinates gain a real sense of the leader and, very importantly, the mission. Conversely, if a leader is aloof or unapproachable, it's more difficult for a subordinate to internalize the mission, or to understand what the leader is all about. This is true in the private sector as well. It's important that people who are part of your organization feel they can ask for advice and— even more vital—that they can make mistakes, and tell you they made them.

The beauty of approachability is that it requires no special gift or skill; indeed, it's a principle that anyone can apply to his everyday life. It's a natural human tendency to be approachable, to seek contact and companionship. I like to link the words *human* and *humor* and not simply because they share the same root. Leaders should be able to share their sense of humor, give and solicit amusing stories, ice breakers if you will, and not think of themselves as holding some exalted position that prohibits them from being themselves or down-to-earth with all ranks.

While it's true that they have more responsibility than those they lead, it's also true that we are all human beings, making this extraordinary journey through life. Each of us shares a common beginning and a common end. So why not keep that in mind? It's not all that difficult to smile when you're doing your MBWA, making the rounds in the morning, just meeting and greeting those who work for you. The truth is, when the men and women who work for you see that the boss is in good humor, they'll get the idea that you're approachable, and they'll feel a little more comfortable saying, "Sir, can I tell you about something?" Just knowing that now and then they can step up and talk to someone who is in a position of leadership is hugely important to subordinates. It helps them to get a sense of what's going on and how they fit in, to feel some ownership in what they're doing, and to have a better understanding of their leaders who are in charge of that mission.

Some young men and women, asked for the first time to shoulder a leader's burden, tend to overreact. Unaccustomed to criticism that flows from two directions (from superiors *and* subordinates), confused about their new roles, and legitimately concerned that any display of cordial behavior will be mistaken for weakness, they are at risk of developing a crusty shell and metamorphosing into a stereotype of the hard, unapproachable leader. This transition has the short-term effect of protecting one from the overt challenges of subordinates, but ultimately results in the leader losing not only the affection of those who work for him but also their loyalty and commitment. And without those two things—loyalty and commitment to a shared cause—failure is inevitable. How do you prevent it? Make yourself approachable.

If your inclination is to say, "I would rather nobody come and see me; I would rather not have to talk with people," then you're not a leader. It's just that simple.

Approachability gives leaders some very important advantages. It allows them to build windows for themselves through which they can gain a clearer understanding of their people, the people who will, to a great extent, determine whether or not the organization runs successfully. A leader is not an oracle though we have all run into some (poor leaders, mostly) who tend to believe they are. We all know the caricature—the boss who issues orders without regard for what's actually happening on the ground, then screams, literally or figuratively, "Go away!" when someone knocks on his door to tell him it can't be done. This type of behavior, which has virtually nothing to do with leadership, seriously degrades the ability of an organization to carry out its mission.

It takes more effort to be approachable, but it's a very human thing. And it flows into compassion (which we'll get to in another chapter), which is an intensely human characteristic. I just don't believe it's natural for someone to be a good leader and be unapproachable at the same time. If your inclination is to say, "I would rather nobody come and see me; I would rather not have to talk with people," then you're not a leader. It's just that simple. You can't be unapproachable and expect to be an effective leader. Folks have to feel that they can talk to you, and you have to exert the effort and make the right moves to build approachability into one of your basic principles of leadership. You can do it.

Approachability also means that I, as the leader, have the ability to approach you. It's a two-way street. If I'm the leader, it's my responsibility to make sure that those open corridors are utilized. Communication is the key to any organization, and approachability is vital to effective communication.

The importance of approachability was never more apparent to me than when I was commandant of cadets at West Point. An outsider might find it surprising to learn that openness—the relatively free expression of ideas between cadets and officers—is a hallmark of the education and training at West Point, and it's not just because the Academy is an academic institution that encourages this interaction. The relationships that officers—from the superintendent to the commandant and on down—maintain with cadets are the most visible examples of building approachability and teaching it by example. There are so many opportunities for interaction—formal and informal—between junior officers and cadets, and leaders make the most of these opportunities to demonstrate the principles of leadership.

The Corps of Cadets is, in a very real sense, part of a large extended family that includes the officers and NCOs who are assigned as their tacs as well as the instructors, professors, and coaches who are integral parts of the Academy's life. Almost all of them can expect a steady stream of cadet traffic through their homes, offices, and workplaces. Leisure time, dinners, and recreational activities are all shared with the cadets. It's a wonderful and important aspect of the Academy because the cadets are officer candidates who are going to be part of the officer corps in a very short time.

It's no accident that we take every opportunity we can at West Point to give cadets face time with the men and women who have been where they are soon going to go. Why? Because leadership is caught as much as it is taught, and we want to give cadets every opportunity we can to catch the leadership principles that they see in their officers. And so if you're practicing these principles of leadership, you'll find that your subordinates will model their behavior on what they see (and what they hear) and eventually internalize these principles.

The point here is that good leaders encourage meaningful interaction between the ranks rather than drawing rigid barriers between them. Their motive is obvious, and it hinges on that principle of approachability—fostering a sense of teamwork and trust that develops new generations of leaders.

The information exchanged in casual encounters can be every bit as valuable, if not more valuable, as information that slides up and down the formal chain of command. Early in my tenure as commandant, I learned that at sometime in the recent past, peanut butter had been removed from the mess hall tables. This might sound like a small thing, but to the cadets it was a disappointing turn of events. An awful lot of cadets liked peanut butter; it was, in fact, a staple of their diet—no doubt a comforting alternative if that day's menu failed to excite them. I would hazard that the taste for peanut butter was universal among the Corps, so it didn't surprise me when I heard it as a serious complaint.

"You know, sir," one of the cadets told me rather sadly, "we used to have peanut butter in the mess hall."

"Really? What happened?"

"I don't know. They just took it away."

"Okay . . . thanks for telling me."

I asked around and found out that peanut butter had indeed been removed from the mess hall, despite its popularity. No one really had an explanation—not even the nutritionist who oversaw the menu—and it was an easy matter for the commandant to decree that peanut butter would henceforth return to the mess hall. The result? To this day I know there are some who remember that I was the commandant who brought peanut butter back to the cadet mess hall. (Everyone's got to be famous for something!) It was a small accomplishment that took very little effort on my part, but it had a profound effect on morale and I became something of a folk hero—not a bad thing for a new leader who's looking to make the right initial impression and wants it to have as wide an audience as possible.

With this one simple gesture, I sent a message that someone way up in the chain of command was willing to listen; someone cared. And that's what soldiers want and deserve—a leader who listens and lets them know that their opinions mean something, and their work is meaningful, understood, and appreciated. Through the simple act of being approachable, leaders can open up the richest fields possible to provide that assurance to their subordinates.

Each of us has the ability to be approachable, but you have to be comfortable in your own skin, and approachability can be exercised in varying degrees. For me, serving as the commandant was an ideal opportunity to use approachability as my strong suit.

First of all, the audience, the Corps of Cadets, was young, impressionable, and eager to learn. From the outset, there is no problem with getting their attention and instilling a sense of junior-senior relationship. Then, by sending them a message of approachability, they are encouraged to feel comfortable exchanging pleasantries, responding to a conversation, or asking for permission to discuss a subject important to them. I had known previous commandants, of course, and each one had his own style of leadership that fit his personality. I mentioned earlier in this book the image I had of the commandant, so adopting a harsh and distant façade would have been completely foreign to who and what I was then and who I am today.

Since I had originally thought the job required more of an iron fist, it was a surprise to find that the position actually played to my strengths. The cadets responded to my natural inclination to be friendly and sympathetic. Again, I don't mean to imply that a leader should be soft or weak. Strength and approachability can coexist. In fact, I believe they are almost always twin characteristics in the strongest leaders. If you're naturally shy or reserved, of course, you'll have to do a bit of extra work to be seen as approachable.

The real problem is the chasm between the cadets and their officers that cadets feel they must respect. But bridging that chasm is not an overwhelming task. That's really the underlying theme of this book: none of these principles is beyond your reach. I'm not suggesting that you have to go to some mythical place where you'll be magically transformed into a great leader. It's not that complicated. You can find your own level; indeed, you'll be an ineffective leader if you're trying to be someone (or something) you're not. There is no pretense with great leaders. They are who they are.

Who among us, for example, could ever aspire to be another Douglas MacArthur or George Patton? By all accounts, General Patton was a hard man who was not naturally approachable. And yet he took opportunities to make himself approachable because he understood its importance. Patton would visit GIs in the hospital; he'd stand out in the middle of a road and direct traffic, and say things to youngsters as they passed by. That was his way of being approachable. To a great extent, it worked—people would say, "Hey, the general was here!" It was effective for him because he did it within his own skills and personality. And if Patton could demonstrate approachability . . . so can you.

General Patton was a hard man who was not naturally approachable. And yet he took opportunities to make himself approachable because he understood its importance.

LEADERSHIP—WORKING WELL WITH OTHERS

Generally speaking, the less approachable you are, the harder your job is going to be. Unapproachable leaders invite anger and hostility, but worse they set themselves up for failure. A large organization, by definition, is comprised of multiple parts, and it's the leader's job to ensure that those parts are synchronized. If the parts are disconnected, the organization cannot run smoothly. Simply put, a leader can't afford to be an island. A central piece of the job description is an ability to work effectively with others—at all levels. There are jobs that can be accomplished quite well by someone who prefers a solitary environment. Scientists, for example, often work alone. So do artists. These can be quiet, lonely endeavors.

But if you choose to be a leader, you are choosing to work with other people. That's the contract. If you want to lead people, you must be approachable. It all comes back to fostering a sense of community and getting people not only to do something they don't necessarily want to do but also to believe that it is the right thing to do and, ultimately, think they're the ones who wanted to do it in the first place.

THE DREADED PERFORMANCE REVIEW

A key component of approachability is counseling. If you are in a position of leadership—whether you are a military officer or a corporate executive—an immensely important part of your job is to review the performances of those beneath you. Too often, though, the performance review becomes an uncomfortable exercise to be endured, producing little of value to either the senior or the subordinate. A performance review should be much more than a perfunctory recitation of pros and cons. It should have more in common with a counseling session than a trip to the principal's office. A performance review involves sitting down with subordinates and communicating with them—it is a dialogue, not a lecture.

Approachability in a leader engenders not only a sense of trust but a sense of respect as well. People value your thoughts and opinions on their performance, and they enjoy having the opportunity to share their feelings. The performance review, when viewed as a counseling session, is a wonderful piece of equipment to have in your leadership toolbox.

In the army, there is also an extremely important responsibility that comes with the performance review because it stands as an official record of the subordinate's performance of specific duties during the rating period and, by extension, an analysis of his potential for the future. Good leaders do their homework ahead of time and establish their ground rules for the session. This should not and need not be an anxiety-provoking encounter. That's why counseling is such an important part of the process.

The performance review, when viewed as a counseling session, is a wonderful piece of equipment to have in your leadership toolbox.

In the army, regular intervals are established for officer efficiency reports, and each person who composes an efficiency report is required to counsel the rated officer within a set time of the end of the reporting period. Unfortunately, that's sometimes a requirement that's passed by pretty brusquely. On many occasions I've had an officer say to me, "You're the first person who ever sat down and talked to me about my efficiency report." What a shame! What a missed opportunity! The performance review coupled with counseling is a chance for the leader not only to point out areas that need improvement but also to let people know that their efforts are appreciated . . . and that he wants to help them be even better. To borrow an apt metaphor, each of us is susceptible to the Peter Principle: we will eventually rise to our own personal level of incompetence. It's inevitable. But that's not something that needs to be emphasized.

Under an approachable leader, there is always the opportunity for growth, and that is the point that needs to be stressed. It's normal and reasonable behavior for someone to try to hide his own shortcomings. But if you've counseled him correctly and developed this approachable attitude, your subordinate is going to say, "Well, you know, I can talk to the old man, and it's not going to destroy me; maybe I'll even be better for it."

That's leadership!

MANAGEMENT BY WALKING AROUND

It should come as no surprise that approachability goes hand in hand with visibility. Obviously, no one will think of you as being approachable if you are holed up in your office all day with the door closed and the shades drawn. This brings us back to the old axiom of MBWA: management by walking around. I spoke with one of my former executive officers not long ago, and we talked about precisely this subject. He said, "You know, the one thing about you was, you were always around. It's like you tried to see almost every one of us every day. We all knew that you were there."

"And was that a good thing?"

He smiled. "Yeah, it sure was."

I had no complicated management plan when I took my walks around. Sometimes it was by Jeep, sometimes by helicopter, but however I got there I was *there*. I just always felt in my heart that being around as many of my subordinates as much as I could, doing something with some of them every day, was the right thing to do, so I would go to their offices or out to their field training or land at their firebases and interact with as many of them as I could every day.

In a week, I would have spent quite a bit of time with a lot of my immediate subordinates and at least a few minutes with many others in the command. I tried to do that not just to stay informed but to let them know that I appreciated their work. Consequently, I developed a comfortable mentoring relationship with these people, each of whom understood that they could talk to me at any time about almost anything.

USE YOUR SENSE OF HUMOR

Incidentally, I know that most everywhere I went, the troops called me *Smilin' Joe*. Part of that was because smiling came easy to me. I'm generally a positive person who finds it natural to look on the bright side of things. But I also understood the value of smiling, of presenting an approachable, upbeat image. I believe people respond to this type of personality far more readily than they do to negativity or pessimism. If you smile at your subordinates, they instantly get the impression that you feel good when you see them, and that, in turn, makes them feel good about themselves. It takes so little effort, and it has such a powerful impact. You don't have to be disingenuous to embrace this philosophy. Again, it's a perfectly human approach to leadership, and it's one that has been a hallmark for me.

What's more, being able to muster an aura of good humor is a key aspect of approachability. You may be surprised to learn that you don't always get together with subordinates to tell them what you want to talk about; more often than not you're there to hear what they want to talk about. And when you do it with an aura of good humor, that human side again, it's amazing what you find out in such circumstances. That's why I consider it one of the basic tenets of leadership falling under the heading of *approachability*. It's something everybody can exercise . . . a naturally human trait. Some are better at it than others, yes, but it's just like any other basic skill: it can be polished and refined. And it's a very effective weapon in the leadership arsenal.

A story about General Alexander Haig helps to illustrate how leaders use their sense of humor to make themselves approachable. In the early fifties, General Haig was a captain and the tactical officer of the cadet company adjacent to the one to which I was assigned. Like most of his colleagues, he was a veteran of the Korean War and held in high esteem by the cadets. He also made it a point to get to know many of us who were not in his direct command.

Twelve years later, he was a colonel back at West Point, serving as deputy commandant of the Corps of Cadets. I was a brand-new major, teaching nuclear engineering and, as one of my extra duties, coaching and mentoring the ski team. (Skiing had been one of my favorite off-duty sports when I was a cadet.) The ski team competed against other teams in the Northeast, which required us to travel in large station wagons, skis piled on top, with cadets and their para-phernalia crowded into the passenger areas. Travel uniforms were strictly mandated, and in cold weather, long overcoats were required. These overcoats were bulky and only useful for standing in forma-tion prior to departure, so before every departure, I found myself imploring Colonel Haig to exempt the ski team from wearing long overcoats. (We compromised: I agreed to request this waiver before every ski team trip, and he agreed to listen to me!)

Fast-forward another ten years, and General Haig was now the supreme allied commander of Europe, the highest military com-mand in the free world. He had also gained world fame from his turbulent days in the White House under President Nixon. I was then serving on the personal staff of Admiral Thomas Moorer, the chairman of the Joint Chiefs of Staff, and traveling to Europe for periodic NATO meetings.

The first time I was there, the chairman sent me to General Haig's headquarters to brief him on assigned matters. While I waited with some trepidation in General Haig's outer office, I recalled our previous encounters, the responsibilities he had car-ried, and the stern, imposing visage I had often seen on the tele-vised news from the past years. Fortunately, his executive officer was an old friend and former football teammate of mine at West Point, so he helped me relax while we chatted about matters past and present. (There are relationships like this beyond number that help us do our business in the army.) When the time came, I walked into General Haig's office, not knowing if he would remember me and unsure of how to start our conversation. I saluted, and the unsmiling general looked up at me and said, "Well, Joe, this is a lot different than arguing about the ski team's uniforms."

Do you think we had an extremely productive and pleasant meeting? You bet we did. Do you think that young colonel ever forgot how the general made himself approachable as a leader? You bet I didn't.

APPROACHABILITY—ESSENTIAL FOR EFFECTIVE COMMUNICATION

Perhaps the most valuable thing about approachability is that it facilitates communication, which, as I've noted, is the lifeblood of any organization; it is an integral part of this mosaic we call leadership. I find that there are basically two ways to obtain information: formally (through the chain of command) and informally (through casual conversation in almost any setting). Interestingly enough, I have discovered that informal communication often results in at least as much valuable information as comes from the official chain of command. A good leader recognizes and respects all paths of communication, and seeks information from every available resource—even those that you might not ordinarily associate with official channels.

For example, in the army, chaplains are an invaluable source of information. Please don't misunderstand: I'm not talking about attempting to secure personal details gleaned through the chaplains' private conversations with soldiers. I'm talking about something more generic. There are men and women of all faiths and all religions in the military, and they often turn to the chaplain in times of difficulty. Not surprisingly, this is particularly true in combat, but it also holds true in peacetime. The troops will say things to a chaplain they may not say to other people; therefore, something that comes back to a leader from the chaplain has to be taken seriously. All information must be viewed with the perspective of where it came from and the circumstances surrounding it, as well as knowledge of the person serving as a conduit. How do you do this? Through approachability and by keeping an open mind.

I once asked a chaplain for help in a complicated situation that involved several junior officers. The chaplain feigned reluctance, and I asked him why. "Because," he said, pointing to the sky, "I'm used to dealing with the top!" Chaplains of all faiths appreciate approachability in leaders because they understand its importance in their own affairs as well.

When I became the commandant at West Point, I found we had established and staffed a counseling center for the cadets. And to be perfectly honest, I wasn't sure how I felt about that when I learned of it. After all, here were these great young cadets, ages seventeen to twenty-four, the very best of their generation, tested, selected, and willing to do better than all the rest. I found myself thinking: *Gee, these are the best young men and women that we can find in America; they volunteered to come here; they are of a quality that sets them apart. Why on earth does anyone think they need a counseling center?* Well, as it turned out, that counseling center was a godsend for more than a few cadets attempting to adjust to a wholly new environment, including the ramifications of a life in the military.

But of equal importance, I soon found that the people in the counseling center—trained psychologists, military officers, and a few civilian assistants—were extremely capable, very well prepared, and enormously thoughtful and compassionate. And at the top of the list, they were the best sources of information on many of the issues I was addressing as the Comm. Again, I'm not talking about the exchange of personal information relating to a specific cadet; I'm talking about overarching issues affecting the Academy community. As with the information I received through casual conversation with the chaplains, information from the counseling center proved invaluable in my efforts to make life at West Point more productive and fulfilling for the cadets.

I also found that the counseling center was headed by Colonel Will Wilson—a former Special Forces officer, a terrific professional, and a Vietnam veteran—who was the son of one of my commanding officers in Germany during my first tour of duty after graduation. The relationships that are woven into one's military experience are among the most unique elements that make the profession of arms in America so rewarding and successful.

The counseling center was (and is) a place where valuable information was exchanged, and it was important for the leadership at West Point to be aware of that information—which, by the way, did not necessarily flow up or filter down through the chain of command. Approachability is the key to obtaining this type of information. A leader has to be aware that not all information is distributed from the CO's office or the conference or boardrooms. Sometimes the most important news is exchanged in less-structured environments. If you want to have access to that news, you'd better be approachable.

We have a saying in the military: you know morale is good if everyone is griping. So this much you can be sure is true: if you want to be a successful leader, you would be well advised to have strong links to the places where the griping gets done.

Sometimes the most important news is exchanged in less-structured environments. If you want to have access to that news, you'd better be approachable.

In other words, you'd better work on your approachability.

8

ADAPTABILITY

Let's be reasonable; do it my way.

—OLD ARMY SAYING

The military is often perceived as a rigid, inflexible universe, one in which orders are followed and the chain of command is unbroken. But that is not always the case; in fact, outsiders would be amazed at the interlocking relationships that really comprise the military chain of command, even more so in today's world of technological marvels. Circumstances are forever changing, and humans have to learn to adapt or find themselves left behind. Yet even with all these new and ever-evolving methods of fire, maneuver, intelligence gathering, and command and control, the leader who fails to recognize that each person under his command is an individual human being, and not merely a cog in the machine, will find success much more difficult, often impossible, to achieve.

The three most important words to a soldier in the U.S. Army are *duty, honor,* and *country. Money* is not one of those words. It's not factored into the equation. But in the private sector? You bet it is.

Encouraging adaptability leads to growth—personal and professional—in subordinates. This is particularly true in the military, but it's also applicable to the business world where often it's the older, more experienced people who are in charge, and if they're not focused on trying to develop the younger folks so they can eventually take over, they're not doing their jobs. It's tougher in industry, I realize, because a person's livelihood is involved: *Some young buck is going to come along and take my place? And I'm supposed to help him? I don't think so!*

The military provides some cushion in this matter, for it requires officers to adapt to new circumstances as they move to different jobs in an organization that has a set structure of rank and mandates new assignments every few years. You can serve a long and fulfilling career, even if you never become a colonel or a general.

The three most important words to a soldier in the U.S. Army are *duty, honor,* and *country. Money* is not one of those words. It's not factored into the equation. But in the private sector? You bet it is. In the military, nobody wonders how much money you're making; it's all laid out right there in army regulations for everyone to see. You're a lieutenant or a captain or a colonel, and the compensation associated with that rank is a matter of public record. In the private sector, except for the highest compensations that must be disclosed in a public company, that information is maintained in confidential corporate files.

In either setting, however, adaptability is a crucial ingredient for success. Adaptability involves being innovative and creative. It doesn't mean you just adapt yourself to something; you also adapt other things to the situation. Oxymoronic as it may sound, the one constant that leaders are always up against is *change*. Changes in terrain, personnel, location, technology, and the enemy are part and parcel of the military experience. Add to that, changes in the human condition, change in social mores, and changes in the political landscape and you've got a potent brew that every leader has to wrestle with. The ability to adapt to all these changes is a crucial part of being an effective leader—keeping your feet, so to speak, when the ground is ever shifting. Just as you begin to feel comfortable—just as you think you have a handle on your leadership role—something will happen that forces you to alter, sometimes dramatically, the way you think and the way you go about your business.

ADAPTABILITY AND VISION

As we look down the road, we'll find that successful adaptability includes having the vision to see what's coming and figuring out how to manage it.

Here's a story about those two interwoven principles of leadership from one of America's greatest athletes, Arthur Ashe. Lieutenant Ashe was assigned to the staff at West Point as an assistant finance officer when I was there teaching nuclear engineering in the mid-sixties. It should be no surprise that he also served as an assistant coach of the cadet tennis team. My wife and I were fortunate to know him through our devotion to regular tennis matches with other members of the staff and faculty.

Fifteen years later, I was the commandant of cadets, and world-famous Arthur Ashe was invited back to West Point to speak to the African American cadets. In his speech to the cadets, he made a point that I remember as if he said it just moments ago: "All of you should be thinking about your futures, and when you do, here is the advice I give to you: get out of the gym, get into the library, and study Spanish!" Arthur Ashe spoke these words in 1980. I would wager that most of the cadets who were fortunate enough to be present still remember that advice.

Arthur Ashe's attempt to implore his audience to adapt to an environment was no easy sell at that turbulent time for African Americans. Those words also invoked the need for courage, confidence, and perseverance to carry through with something that his listeners might not ordinarily take to heart, given their backgrounds. We'll see these principles in later chapters.

Leadership inspires "followership," and Arthur Ashe's speech in 1980 was telling the African American cadets who were present that when they had an opportunity that would require them to adapt to take full advantage of it. Again, the principles of leadership overlap and intertwine to make the whole leader. In a clear sense, this was a case where adaptability and vision came together as principles. They do relate to one another, and in fact they are dependent on one another. It's wonderful to have vision, to be a forward-thinking leader, but it doesn't do you any good if you can't adapt to what the vision says is going to happen. Certainly, there is no shortage of people who can see the train coming at them, barreling down the tracks, and yet find themselves incapable of action even with the prospect of an imminent collision. For them, the idea of adaptability in leadership is not ingrained.

No two situations are ever the same, so adapt to the one you find yourself in and move out.

Adaptability is part of the equation. Everybody is different. That's one of the things we all understand. Consider the military world. Under your command are Lieutenant Jones, Lieutenant Smith, and Lieutenant Brown. They are all second lieutenants, all with the same rank and equivalent duties. Yet each of them is unique and should be treated as unique. Trying to fit every individual into a set mold is a formula for failure. All should feel they are being treated equally—that the playing field is level and you are being fair to each of them. But your leadership role when dealing with these three officers is not only to adapt to each one of them but also to get them to adapt to a single leader.

A leader's primary job is to build a team, a creative endeavor that requires enormous adaptability. In the army, that's something I always tried to encourage in subordinates: the exchange of ideas and the freedom to do things differently. *No two situations are ever the same, so adapt to the one you find yourself in and move out.* As I've said repeatedly, the army is often viewed as a rigid and narrow organization, but that really isn't the case. Certainly, I never found rigidity and narrowness to be the most effective in leading men and women of all ranks, creeds, and colors. There are sets of instructions, written or implied (through tradition) for just about any task—in the military or private sector. And there will always be people who will insist upon following the instructions to the point of failure—and beyond.

ENCOURAGING INNOVATION

A good leader encourages innovation, adapting to the situation. And that has a great multiplier effect: it encourages subordinates to use their creativity and ingenuity. That's important because subordinates will not be subordinates forever—you are, after all, responsible for developing new leaders among your many duties, so you want to give subordinates the idea that they can be creative, make innovations, and do things better through their own unique skills and knowledge. I have been around long enough to see that all of today's standard operating procedures in the army have evolved from ideas that subordinates adapted from other existing systems.

I would understand if you did not know that West Point is a place where thinking occurs "outside the box." Even those of us who have passed through the gray stone walls of West Point like to joke that the Academy's motto is: "Two hundred years of tradition uninterrupted by progress." The reality is something else entirely. We at

West Point are in the business of training and educating leaders, and the seeds of the principles espoused on these pages are planted and nurtured from the first day new cadets arrive on the Plain. Over the years, I have found that opportunities are embraced to varying degrees, but the most promising leaders tend to be the ones who are willing to be innovative, adapting to the situation and taking chances when their judgment tells them it's the right thing to do. They become the young officers who are willing to say, "What can I do to make my troops better at what they do, and make my platoon more effective?"

Similarly, when new lieutenants demonstrate innovation, they have to be rewarded and recognized. The good company commander doesn't chastise a platoon leader, one of his lieutenants, for not seeking permission to think outside the box; rather, he compliments the lieutenant for his creativity. But what happens if the lieutenant's adaptability backfires—if the decision turns out to be a bad one? Well, if you're a good leader, other principles of leadership enter, and you take that on with a sense of duty as well as thoughtful compassion. You certainly do not stand up in front of everybody and say, "Lieutenant, that was a dumb idea! What were you thinking?"

While mistakes must be addressed and sheer overzealousness has to be reined in and channeled in positive directions, you have to take care not to inflict permanent damage to the record or the psyche of a young person who has really tried to do something that he thought was good and unique.

If that occurs to you, I'd advise you to read the chapter on compassion with particular care. Then think how an alternative approach like this might work for you: you make time for a separate counseling session, and you ask the lieutenant, calmly and without accusation, "What do you think went wrong? What did you have in mind?" *All* good leaders who rise to positions of responsibility are alert to their obligation to facilitate growth and confidence in their subordinates, and that doesn't happen by giving a public reprimand to every subordinate who is willing to take a chance to accomplish the mission.

Any form of leadership that's encouraging adaptability and innovative behavior is going to encounter obstacles and missteps—places where people make mistakes. The idea is not to abdicate responsibility or encourage subordinates to usurp authority or ignore protocol. It goes without saying that there are rules and regulations within any organization, and the army has more than its fair share. That said, even in a military environment, and certainly in a civilian environment, there are opportunities for growth and innovation, and the young leader who shows an aptitude for adaptability has to be granted some leeway to succeed or to fail. While mistakes must be addressed and sheer overzealousness has to be reined in and channeled in positive directions, you have to take care not to inflict permanent damage to the record or the psyche of a young person who has really tried to do something that he thought was good and unique.

ADAPTABILITY: THE ARMY VERSUS THE CORPORATE WORLD

Perhaps because the stakes are higher in the military—we are, after all, in the business of protecting the country—I find in today's army that in every situation we think of subordinates as human beings, rather than as spokes in the wheel. I don't mean to denigrate how civilian businesspeople treat their employees; after all, I've been a corporate boss as well. But the army really does try to look carefully at its people as real assets. They're not interchangeable, disposable parts.

In business, perhaps, you don't quite have the same human relationships as are found in the military. That's curious, too, because in business it's not unusual for employees to work closely together for many years, whereas in the military you might have two or three years together at most before reassignment forces a separation. You'd almost think that this high turnover would hinder the development of strong relationships, but in my experience, the reverse is true. One possible explanation for this is the very strong similarity in lifestyle enjoyed by everyone in the military. We work together and in many instances live together on the same base or in the same military housing area. We live within the same system of reassignment and rotation that trains us for the exigencies of war. As a result, relationships develop that help us understand the changes that we make to adapt to changing circumstances and changing times.

The military, by necessity, looks closely and constantly at the growth potential of its leaders. And there is a clear path to be followed—for everyone: I'm a private today, a corporal tomorrow, a command sergeant major twenty years from now, and on it goes; or "from bars to stars" as they say for the officer corps. Your leaders only have you for two or three years in the army, and then you're moving someplace else. Good military leaders understand that they must train someone to take their job, and they act accordingly. For everyone, up and down the ranks, that's okay; that's the way it's supposed to be. As a military leader (and I think the private sector could really learn from this model), I need to have the kind of confidence that allows me to say, "Yup, it's time for me to move on."

Building within yourself the capability to adapt to these circumstances will help you understand how best to handle young subordinates who must be trained in the craft of leadership. In reality,

I do believe this same adaptability has to be applied in the business world as well; after all, none of us has figured out how to get younger. We are all making the same journey, regardless of the route. Eventually you, Mr. or Ms. CEO, will hand over the keys to the corner office, and when that time comes, there had better be someone ready to take your place.

Your leaders only have you for two or three years in the army, and then you're moving someplace else. Good military leaders understand that they must train someone to take their job, and they act accordingly.

The entire structure of the military revolves around this promotional leadership model; whereas, in the civilian world it's a far less egalitarian process. In the private sector, you pick and choose the people you want for all kinds of reasons. And perhaps the greatest difference of all: if you can't find a suitable person within your business to take the top job, well, then you just go out on a search, often with a headhunter to help, and hire a new CEO. It seems simple enough, but in reality it is a much more complex and risky task than selecting new commanders for the army at all levels.

It's unfortunate that the business world does not readily embrace the military's adaptability and do more to encourage building from within. There are exceptions, like a company's size or business model that would prohibit this approach, but the civilian world's conventional wisdom seems to point to hiring senior leaders from outside the organization.

That said, adaptability remains a key principle to being a leader in the commercial world because things are going to change. The market will change, products and technology will change, people will change, and you—as a manager or CEO—have to be able to adapt to those changes.

Here's a real-world, up-to-date example of what I'm talking about when I say adaptability is a principle of good leadership. When I first went into private business, living in Madrid, Spain, one of the primary modes of local and international communication was the Teletype, an ungainly machine that noisily converted an electronic message into printed words on a paper tape. Then along came this really neat piece of technology called a fax machine that used a great new innovation: heat-sensitive paper that transferred words from electronic symbols to written text. And you could use this to transmit actual documents from Spain to almost every other country in the world. Sometimes the words would be a little blurry, but still . . . what a revolutionary technological advancement! It wasn't long before I took my Teletype machine and tossed it in the trash can.

Everything changes. Either you can be dragged kicking and screaming into the new world . . . or you can adapt and lead the way.

It wasn't long after that, there was a fax machine that printed on real paper, so the words didn't fade with time, the way they did on heat-sensitive paper. And today? The Internet and e-mail have taken over. Hardly anyone uses a fax machine in the commercial business world anymore. Now you scan everything, even signatures, into electronic signals and transmit it through e-mail. What's more, it costs far less because you don't have to rent a telephone line to use e-mail. It wasn't that long ago when hardly anyone had even heard of the word *Internet,* but today it is responsible for a "sea change" in the way the world communicates and conducts business. And so how could you possibly expect to be a leader in today's environment if you couldn't adapt to use this technological advancement in your leadership responsibilities?

Everything changes. Either you can be dragged kicking and screaming into the new world . . . or you can adapt and lead the way. While I would never go so far as to suggest that everything I've laid out from my personal experience is now part of the West Point curriculum, I do think it's fair to say that each of these principles helps shape the cadet's experience and development. Certainly, a major component of the educational experience at West Point involves placing challenges—some expected, some thoroughly unexpected—in front of a cadet and seeing how he responds. Leadership potential can be gauged by watching these young men and women adapt to their circumstances and surroundings; the degree to which they are willing to cast aside convention and demonstrate initiative is a reflection of their innate adaptability.

IT'S NOT JUST ABOUT MOVING UP THE LADDER

One caveat regarding adaptability: if subordinates or employees get the idea that the primary motivation for your creativity, ingenuity, and adaptability is self-serving (i.e., a shameless attempt to get promoted), it will most assuredly undercut your effectiveness and theirs as well. Granted, some folks get away with this approach. They're highly ambitious, and they can become successful because they've got this "how I can move up the ladder" focus: I want to be a company commander, so I can get this job, then that job, and so on. There's no doubt that some people work that way, and they are successful up to a point. I don't buy it, and I would urge that you not buy it either. I guess I just never had the ambition or the self-interest or whatever it takes to behave that way. For me, it was always about performing the task at hand to the best of my ability at any given time. Whatever the task, that's what I did. I never asked for a particular assignment, and I never refused one that was assigned to me. Period.

If you are committed to the job and to providing an atmosphere of encouragement and growth for those who are under your command, success will find its way to you.

It never really occurred to me that if I was a good company commander, I might get selected to be a battalion commander; it just seemed too distant to be of any great concern. Nonetheless, moving up the ladder does come in large part from innovation and adaptability. So my recommendation to any young leader is this: use your powers to adapt and be creative, and don't worry about what's in it for you somewhere around the bend; worry about what's in front of you right now. Do the best job you can, rather than looking for the next promotion. I don't mean to imply that you shouldn't be using your vision or be ambitious and careful about your career. But I do believe that if you are committed to the job and to providing an atmosphere of encouragement and growth for those who are under your command, success will find its way to you. Recognition comes to those who are patient and committed to their work and mindful of those who work for them. Some people can get away with self-promotion; for most of us, however, selflessness is by far the purer and more reliable strategy.

ENTHUSIASM ENCOURAGES ADAPTABILITY

It may seem contradictory to say one should live in the moment and concentrate on the task at hand, while simultaneously exercising adaptability and foresight. But you shouldn't ignore what's going on in the world around you. Good leaders are forever studying, looking, and learning, but they avoid the trap of doing things merely to get noticed. It's about enthusiasm, which is almost always a necessary companion to adaptability.

Adapting means changing, but what you find so often is that people become very comfortable in their roles. They are accustomed to doing things a certain way, and all of a sudden, new circumstances or a new boss is shaking their comfortable world. The natural response is for people to feel trepidation. In my experience, the enthusiasm that a leader brings to those circumstances is a great lubricator; it reassures people that change can be good and not necessarily painful. If the boss says, "We're all in this together, we can adapt to it, and we can make it work!" that little shot of personal enthusiasm can have a tremendous calming influence.

A leader's enthusiasm encourages adaptability in subordinates, and the two combined can be nothing less than inspirational. When we made the transition to an all-volunteer army, it was critical that we recognize the importance of making military service desirable. We had to find a way to adapt the army to something that young men and women would be inspired to join—as opposed to the traditional image of an institution that drafted people who did not always want to serve—and then, hopefully, convince some of them to stay.

No doubt there is a lot of convincing that goes on even today after one joins the army or any of the armed forces, but more to the point is adapting to make the situation one where leadership works. And leadership works best when people are doing something they believe they want to do. That is the focus of the leadership of the army today, and I believe it translates exactly into the business world as well. It's all part of adapting because we're really talking about taking youngsters and teaching them first of all to be followers, and then educating, training, and inspiring them to be our future leaders.

ADAPTABILITY WITHOUT FORMALITY

One of the most effective ways to make this formula work is to use informal situations where you simply shoot the breeze. I already mentioned that while I was the commandant at West Point, we created ethical doughnuts. There was a period every Saturday morning when most cadets were free from classes and other duties, and during this window there was an opportunity for cadets to gather in the company's day room, an area furnished for seating and conversation with a very informal atmosphere, where cadets could get together and have a chance to talk. Obviously, if the commandant wanted to come and talk to the company, I'd come and talk. But we tried to make it so it wasn't coercive; cadets could wander in or out at their leisure, have a doughnut and a cup of coffee, partake in the conversation, or merely listen. (Remember Schweitzer's formulation of *ethics*.) The cadets themselves ended up calling our sessions *ethical doughnuts* because we often wound up talking about human behavior.

Ethical doughnuts was a great forum; it required me to adapt to a variety of situations and conversations with the cadets, almost always with their tactical officers and tac NCOs present. It also increased their awareness of my approachability: here I am with just about twenty or thirty guys and gals, and we're sitting around having a cup of coffee, talking about stuff, and I'm clever enough to be able to get just about any of them to ask me a question. Then I actually answer the question.

Adaptability is a lot more than just walking up and shaking hands and saying hello to new people—it's one of creating personal behavior that gives people a sense of comfort so that they can ask a question knowing they won't be derided or ridiculed, and wonder of wonders, there's an answer that turns out to be really helpful. I won't forget to throw them a little "attaboy" for asking; there's a way in almost every instance to do that when someone asks a question. It's all about enjoying what you're doing, being a leader, and exercising that good old principle: adaptability.

Adaptability, as you can probably tell, overlaps with many of the principles we've been talking about. With ethical doughnuts it was approachability and just another way to foster dialogue outside the traditional chain of command. There are many others, and you can adapt them to fit your own situation. An officer on the rifle range can chat with soldiers almost any time while they're training. He can walk through the barracks at night. A manager in the private sector can leave his corner office and visit laboratories or production departments. Admittedly, since almost everyone in the business world goes home at night, such interaction requires a bit more creative thinking than in the military. But that doesn't mean it can't be done. It just takes effort . . . and adaptability.

FROM MANAGEMENT TO LEADERSHIP

As long as we're defining terms, this is as good a place as any to address the fundamental issue of leadership versus management. Are they interchangeable? Are they synonymous? Not really. I don't think anyone doubts that good leadership involves an element of inspiration that is not necessarily associated with good management. Managerial skills tend to be thought of as mechanical—a good manager knows the business well; he can create efficient logistical systems and is good at handling things as opposed to handling people. The two are not necessarily divided, but they are separable. A good manager, ultimately, has to become somewhat skilled in leadership because there are going to be people underneath that manager who need to be led, not just managed. *Things* are managed; *people* are led. Making the transition from manager to leader involves a significant amount of adaptability.

Adaptability is a principle any aspiring leader should eagerly embrace, for leadership, by definition, involves guiding people across an ever-changing landscape. Consider again the military. If you're an officer, leadership will be a part of your life from beginning to end. You start with a platoon, as I did, then a company command, a battalion command, a brigade command, and if you're lucky, a division command. To put that in more concrete, numerical terms, you're going from an organization of some forty or fifty people to an organization of some fifteen *thousand* people. At every level you're basically starting over, learning to perform specific tasks for the first time.

Things are managed; people are led. Making the transition from manager to leader involves a significant amount of adaptability.

That's what assuming the increasing responsibilities that go with the mantle of leadership is really all about: being able to effectively adapt as you move from one level to the next. It's a principle that you have to be able to internalize and take on because it not only allows you to perform your new duties but also transmits subliminally to your subordinates the importance of being able to adapt to a situation.

Comparatively speaking, I haven't spent all that much time in the corporate world, and I certainly didn't start at the bottom and work my way up, the way I did in the military (the way everyone does in the military), but I believe nevertheless that all these same principles apply, most certainly adaptability.

Adaptability is a principle any aspiring leader should eagerly embrace, for leadership, by definition, involves guiding people across an ever-changing landscape.

In the corporate world, different skill sets are required for the innumerable and variegated jobs that are found in the private sector. In a certain sense, management responsibility is given to each individual for managing a finite portion of a profit-making or nonprofit organization and making it run efficiently. The similarities between the corporate and military world are ones of adapting to something that's going to be changing, sometimes not very rapidly, and sometimes, it seems, almost with the speed of light.

ADAPTING TO THE COMPETITION

The primary difference on the corporate side, as I have experienced it, was that we were dealing with a highly competitive environment that rewarded success and punished failure in a very real, monetary way almost every day. And we had to report with detailed explanations to our public (the company's shareholders) every quarter on our progress. At Frequency Electronics, we are involved in extraordinarily high-end technology, and there just aren't very many competitors. As a result, most everybody knows each other, and in a situation like that, there's a keener sense of competition—not only for business but also in terms of figuring out what our customers are going to need, which direction technology and our competitors may be going, and figuring out what we should be doing about it. It's a constant struggle to determine whether or not there's a better way to get the job done than what we are already doing.

ADAPTING TO MEET THE ENEMY

There is competition in the military, too, of course, but of a very different sort. Within the military, there is enormous teamwork and no competition for business. Our opponent is the enemy of our country, who threatens our freedoms and our democratic way of life. Our strategy looks across the globe, determining through intelligence what our enemies may have planned. With that outlook, our mission becomes one of preparing to meet and defeat that enemy. But before and beyond meeting and defeating, our strategy will center on deterrence. Better to protect our country with strength that deters an enemy than to actually go to war. The life we lead in the military is one of service to a peacetime mission of deterrence, but with preparation for war should that ever come.

Within the military, there is enormous teamwork, and no competition for "business." Our opponent is the enemy of our country, who threatens our freedoms and our democratic way of life.

Here's a story about military equipment and how it relates to adaptability and preparation for war. The rifle obviously has been the basic infantry weapon for centuries. When I joined the army in 1951, the rifle of choice was the 30-caliber M1 30-06. A heavy, nine-pound repeating rifle developed during World War II, it was admired especially by great marksmen, who found that the M1 could hit and destroy targets at distances of more than a thousand yards.

When that war ended, and as our requirements for future wars adjusted, the United States became part of NATO. As a member of NATO, we adopted a rifle that was a NATO-developed weapon: the M-14, which had been produced by a Belgian firm. As part of the cooperative NATO structure in those early days, we had agreed to use equipment developed by each other's military. The M-14 was essentially a new and improved version of the M-1.

We had it in our inventory and trained our soldiers on it, but as Vietnam began to heat up in the sixties, we found that the M-14 simply did not work well in the environment of Southeast Asia. First of all, it was particularly susceptible to the heat, humidity, rain, and mud of the jungles; second, it was heavy, and under such arduous climactic conditions, fatigue became a big factor; third, the M-14 was a weapon best suited to shooting at longer range, but our soldiers in Vietnam frequently found themselves in close combat, at ranges of less than a few dozen yards.

So the M-14 was deemed problematic, if not an outright failure, for service in Southeast Asia. Fortunately, Colt had developed a weapon called the M-16: a smooth, reliable rifle whose operating mechanism was much more adaptable to the environment we were in—mud, heat, humidity—although nothing would work well in that environment if it was not kept clean.

The M-16 was smaller caliber, but it fired a very high velocity round that was much more effective at the ranges we engaged in Vietnam. It was also much lighter than the M-14 and proved to be a terrific weapon, representative of the willingness and capability of today's army to adapt to the demands of modern warfare. It also shows that to make the most of our research and development budget—which, after all, represents a significant portion of the military's spending—adaptability is also an absolute necessity. As the Scottish poet Robert Burns wrote (and the American novelist John Steinbeck, adapted in *Of Mice and Men*), ". . . The best-laid schemes o' mice an' men Gang aft agley . . ."*

---

*You can access the complete poem "To A Mouse, On Turning Her Up In Her Nest With The Plough" by Robert Burns at http://www. robertburns.org.

A paramount responsibility of government is the national defense. Our national government is solely responsible for this solemn duty, and that is accomplished through the armed forces—the business I was in for so long. Our national security is made up of many important and interdependent elements, but defense is the business of professionals, and we are dead serious about our business.

While the stakes obviously are not as high, competition abounds in the business environment, and that makes adaptability utterly essential to viability. The battle is ceaseless in the civilian world; the field is forever changing and shifting, and the competition is the opponent. That's the other side of the equation. If you are running a business in the private sector, you have allies and friendly acquaintances—partners who regularly team up to compete together for business; customers, suppliers, and the like—but you also have competition. You are competing for not only the resources of your suppliers but also the business of the customers. It's sometimes polite but always demanding and energetic, and at times there can be very serious competition that threatens your very existence.

Our national security is made up of many important and interdependent elements, but defense is the business of professionals, and we are dead serious about our business.

In either environment, though, you will find that the ability to adapt as the world changes around you will serve you well in your role as a leader. As I found myself rising through the chain of command in the army, it never occurred to me to be concerned about attaining the next promotion. Just as in younger days, I was always focused on what I was expected to do *now* . . . and not on what might come next. I tried to concentrate on the job at hand and adapt myself to each new demand.

Aspiring to the highest rank possible is not all that's important. You should also aspire to be the best you can be at the rank you're already in. Be prepared to adapt to the changes—those you know are coming and those you don't—do your job, do it with enthusiasm and diligence and creativity, and you will naturally find your way to the next level.

Aspiring to the highest rank possible is not all that's important. You should also aspire to be the best you can be at the rank you're already in.

9

COMPASSION

There is only one unpardonable sin.
—FROM THE SHORT STORY,
"THE UNPARDONABLE SIN" BY JAMES P. WOOD

More than a quarter century ago when I became commandant of cadets at West Point, I was asked to write an introduction to *Bugle Notes,* the handbook annually dispensed to all incoming cadets, the new plebes. *Bugle Notes* contains everything the new cadet is expected to know about life at the Academy—all the "Plebe Poop," as it's affectionately known. Some of the information in *Bugle Notes* must be committed to memory, like Schofield's Definition of Discipline or Scott's Fixed Opinion or the number of days until graduation. Other material is included simply to enlighten and inform the young cadet, to help in his transition from the freewheeling days of high school to the far more rigorous and demanding environment of the U.S. Military Academy.

In the commandant's introduction to *Bugle Notes,* I composed an open letter to the plebes in which I asked them to reflect on what they expected of their education at West Point and to establish in their own minds precisely what types of leaders they wanted to become. I highlighted the words *tough, compassionate,* and *understanding.* Of these, *compassionate* is perhaps the most difficult to internalize even though compassion is an intensely human characteristic. It's also one that has to be factored into leadership. I'll repeat that: *it has to be factored into leadership.* If you're lacking in compassion, you will eventually lose both the respect and admiration of your subordinates, and in their place you'll find an atmosphere of fear and mistrust. To me, exercising compassion means you understand that there is a fine line between being too tough and being too soft. The effective leader must find a balance between the two, exercising the strength required to maintain good order, while simultaneously understanding the need to account for human frailties.

Compassion is a principle; toughness and understanding are characteristics, things you can employ in order to get decisions made and jobs completed in a timely and efficient manner. Compassion is a principle of action that I feel is right in the middle of this whole consideration of the principles of leadership. A leader must be tough-minded—there is no question about that. Anyone who has been a boss, on any level, understands the challenges associated with managing real people doing hard jobs. Moving up the leadership scale, transitioning from junior officer to senior commander, or from hourly wage worker to salaried manager, is not to be taken lightly; it is a daunting proposition. No one should be surprised to discover that the higher the ascent on the leadership ladder, the more difficult and complicated the job becomes.

I recall vividly one young cadet who had violated a number of rules and was generally just behaving so poorly that he eventually found himself facing the commandant with the possibility of being discharged from the Academy. He was not, however, without positive characteristics; in fact, he was an intelligent young man, though somewhat immature, who clearly possessed some strong leadership capabilities. I tried to take that into account when he was finally brought before me for this most serious of disciplinary actions.

"Son, you have violated the rules to the point where you're going to be discharged from the Corps," I said. "But if you behave, and do the right thing, you could earn yourself the opportunity to come back to West Point next year. I'll leave the door open, but whether you make it back is ultimately up to you." Not only did he return and graduate with the class that came to West Point the year after he did, he served the army well and today is the chief executive officer of an important new corporation in Washington, D.C. We had dinner together not long ago—I hadn't seen him in years—and he told me that rarely a day goes by that he doesn't reflect on that day in my office and what it meant to him.

It's very rewarding when your decisions turn out like that, and I'm pleased that life has been good to this fine man. But I also know that things could have turned out differently. So how can you ever be sure that one young person might be worth a second chance? More often than not, the record brings you to a point when everything is weighed in your mind and your heart, and you take a chance and go with what you might call *gut instinct*. That's where your heart comes in.

Among the prerequisites for a good leader is a thickening of the skin. Sorry, but there is no way around that one. It is the leader's lot in life to be the subject of speculation and second-guessing among contemporaries and subordinates at every level.

In the case of the young man I just described, he had spent two years at the Academy developing some terrific skills and capabilities, but he just had not been confronted with responsibility for his own actions. He needed time away, to grow up. So he went back to his home, went to another college for a year, and then came back to graduate from West Point. And it worked out well for all sides. The fact is that almost every duty of leadership that requires decision making will require weighing competing views and cutting through the fog of unknowns and unknowables. Experiences like this will sharpen the human instinct for compassion that all good leaders have.

Among the prerequisites for a good leader is a thickening of the skin. Sorry, but there is no way around that one. It is the leader's lot in life to be the subject of speculation and second-guessing among contemporaries and subordinates at every level. As I noted in chapter 7, in the army we know morale is good when everyone is griping. In any organization there will be people with varying degrees of skill and aptitude, demonstrating varying degrees of pleasure and displeasure with their jobs. One of your more important tasks, as their leader, is to keep their attitudes in harmony with doing the best job they are capable of doing. But this is a never-ending struggle, contested over constantly shifting terrain. To put it in military terms, it's a battle that is won many times over, but the campaign never ends.

TOUGH HAS A HEART

A leader who lacks toughness, with all that implies—a thick skin, a willingness to adapt to the situation and make difficult decisions, the courage to do what is right and not what is easiest—will not be a leader for long. A leader must also find a way to develop that toughness without sacrificing heart and soul. Human beings are not machines—you can't simply throw a switch and expect them to work at uniformly high levels, with a common degree of enthusiasm and excitement. Nor can you expect that swift kicks to the behind are the answer to all of your leadership problems. We are all different, and we respond to different motivations. A leader's job is to figure out how to get the most out of the people who work for him; to do that, you have to know your people. You have to reach out to them; you have to mentor them. Again, you're not supposed to be their best friend. But neither is it written anywhere that you are required to be their enemy. Indeed, the boss who has not earned the respect and affection of his subordinates has little chance of succeeding as their leader, and there is virtually no chance that their organization will reach the levels of achievement of which it is capable.

I remember walking around one day many years ago out at our motor pool in the Twenty-fifth Infantry Division, just doing what I did every day to stay in touch with the troops. There was the usual beehive of activity—youngsters working on tanks and other vehicles, making small repairs, going about the daily business of military life. All of a sudden I heard one of the men cut loose with a stream of expletives (a perfectly normal and human reaction to having painfully banged his knuckles when a bolt broke loose). He was still seething and shouting when our eyes met. Red-faced and embarrassed, he instantly fell silent. I don't know if he had ever heard me say anything before on profanity, but he offered me a sheepish, "Sorry, sir."

There are two ways to handle a situation like this. You can lecture a soldier for improper behavior—"What would your mother think?" and the like. Or you can recognize the situation for what it really is—an unintended yelp of discomfort—and try to pass it off to the benefit of all parties. So I smiled at the young soldier and said simply, "Makes you feel better, doesn't it, son?"

He nodded, laughed, and went back to work. And so did everyone else: You know, the old man's okay. He knows what works and what doesn't.

I could have given that soldier a lecture right there on the spot, in front of his buddies. To what end, though? He meant no harm or disrespect. The situation was easily diffused with a dose of humor. That was the compassionate thing to do. You see, putting on a tough façade or acting as if you have an iron fist is not always necessary. You have to find your own path to leadership and your own style of management; however, I believe that for all human beings, the natural way to lead is with compassion. Think about it: compassion requires thoughtfulness for others, and if they know you are thoughtful of them, you'll find them reciprocating in spades. In reality, it's often easier to use an iron fist than to use your compassion, act tougher rather than act more human. But I honestly don't feel you can be a good leader if you have no sense of compassion.

Compassion provides balance for leaders of all kinds and at all levels, and also for those they guide. Subordinates need to understand that you are in charge, and that your decisions must be respected and honored. But they also need to feel that you care about them—as subordinates, as key members of the organization, and as human beings. Time and again the challenge for a young leader is developing control over the sometimes conflicting emotions involved in this balancing act. When you're looking at something from a compassionate viewpoint, a sympathetic reaction can be quite normal. But compassion does not always evoke sympathy. Compassion can also evoke revulsion. It can work both ways. So how do you balance that?

A part of the answer, at least, can be traced back to Schofield's Definition of Discipline:

> The discipline which makes the soldiers of a free country reliable in battle is not to be gained by harsh or tyrannical treatment . . .

To me, Schofield's Definition of Discipline remains as vital today as it was on the day it was composed, more than 130 years ago. It argues, quite persuasively, that while a leader must be strong and confident, he is not to wield his power indiscriminately without regard for the vital needs of subordinates—or peers either for that matter. Whether in the military or the private sector, a title of authority carries with it great responsibility, and that responsibility is not to be taken lightly. A leader would be wise to let Schofield's Definition serve as a guiding principle in all that he does. Central to the Definition is the idea of compassion. I think Schofield is saying that a true barometer of great leadership is the ability to demonstrate compassion. If compassion does not inform your leadership, then you really aren't going to be much of a leader at all.

But it goes even deeper than that. Schofield reminds us that leadership is not about harsh or tyrannical treatment, and that indelible message is meant for leaders and subordinates alike. It's important that everyone within the organization recognizes that we are all fallible creatures; we all need certain types of human relationships. By modeling the concept of compassion, leaders establish an overarching philosophy within their organizations and at the same time implant that key sense of community. *We're all in this together.* Simply put: if you treat subordinates well, they are likely to treat each other well. And, in turn, they will be more inclined to work hard for you, to do all they can to keep you aware of what's going on, and to seek out and value your approval.

COMPASSION IS PERSONAL

As a principle to be transmitted, compassion is most effective on a personal, individual basis as opposed to something that can be applied to an entire unit. A unit can have perseverance, for example, but an individual has compassion. You can talk about having compassion for a group of people, but in that sense it should be applied carefully, and it should not be casually manipulated.

For example, it might be tempting to say that if we can express compassion for a group, then similarly, we can express displeasure with that same group. Taken one step further, a proponent of this philosophy might argue that group punishment is the most effective type of punishment. We're all familiar with this type of strategy: somebody in the company has violated a rule, so the entire company is placed on restriction. This style of leadership has been known for centuries and has been shown to be counterproductive to all good performance but, sadly, is still around in some arenas even today. The rather primitive idea is that group punishment fosters unity and encourages the unit to police itself. As far as I'm concerned, however, this type of behavior is anathema to good leadership. It's a cliché that it discourages unit cohesiveness; it is, rather, more likely to foster intense resentment and hostility toward the offending party and can lead to inappropriate or even violent acts of retribution.

Anyone who approves of such chaotic and primitive behavior should reconsider his role as a leader. Far from promoting unity, group punishment has a divisive effect: the group knows there is somebody who has done something wrong, and its being punished because of that person. So in all likelihood, they ride that person out of the group—one way or another. And what's the next thing? Where do you go from there? A leader who encourages a group to police itself, vigilante style, has basically abdicated all responsibility. It's a totally errant form of leadership.

Now let's turn it around and look at the inverse of this scenario. Say, for example, that a unit in training has some kind of terrible experience. Maybe there's an accident, and one person is killed and several others injured. In that instance, a leader would be well advised to think of compassion in terms of the entire group, and not just on an individual basis. The entire unit might be given time off; special counseling might be considered. Regardless of how it is manifested, group compassion could, and should, be exercised. But it does not work the other way. Group compassion is sensible and utterly human (and humane); group punishment is illogical and self-defeating.

In point of fact, however, this intensely human characteristic of compassion, comprised of both sympathy and revulsion, is something that is more readily and efficiently exercised on an individual basis. Why? Because in exercising compassion, you are trying to convey to subordinates that indeed there is something inside the old man besides a heart of stone. It shows that you are more than just a uniform with an insignia of rank (if you are in the military) or a suit and tie (if you are in the business world). You are not just the boss. You are a human being, too, and the same temptations and foibles that can affect anyone in your workforce are right there in front of you as well. And as a human being who is also their leader, you understand that there are occasions when good old human *compassion* is warranted.

Group compassion is sensible and utterly human (and humane); group punishment is illogical and self-defeating.

I do not mean to cast compassion as something that should be exercised in a calculated, self-promoting way. Follow your heart as well as your head on these matters. Listen to your conscience. A good leader grows instincts about what is right and what is wrong and intuitively uses compassion when it might serve a greater purpose than punishment. I am simply trying to point out that there is a common-sense component to all of this: a leader who understands when compassion is needed is a better leader—and a better human being. So why not use this tool, which is so readily available?

Compassion is an invaluable principle of leadership. It adds depth and nuance to your image and skills as a leader, promoting you as someone who is not just a soulless, hard-nosed guy who may be able to lead troops through battle. I believe that a compassionate leader is the one who truly commands the support and respect of his troops. They follow him not only because they are acting under his orders but also because they believe in him—and they don't want to disappoint him.

Compassion can take many forms; it can include acts large and small. Regardless, if handled properly, the end result is almost always a strengthening of the bond between leader and subordinate. But it can also lead to unintended consequences, and all of us who carry the authority of leadership need to keep that in mind. Let me share with you a little story about my tenure as company commander while stationed in Germany as the Cold War was really beginning to heat up. We took regular trips from the western region of the country where I was stationed over to the East German border, where one of our major training areas was located. It was a deployment where we went in by convoy, so we'd usually leave early in the morning and arrive late the same evening or early the next morning.

It was a long journey, and it always began with my Jeep driver arriving to pick me up at our apartment before sunup, usually around 0500 hours. He was a very pleasant and earnest young man, as likable as any soldier I've ever known. On this particular morning, I had invited him to join my wife and me for breakfast. To me, that was an act of compassion because we were leaving before the mess hall opened, and he would have had to travel on whatever food he had bought from the PX beforehand. My wife had cooked up a big meal of bacon, eggs, toast, coffee, and juice—perfect for fueling up for a long trip. I don't recall the topic of conversation although I vividly remember saying to my wife, as I often did almost absent-mindedly, "Eat your crust." Now, this may sound kind of silly, but I was always very attentive to whether my wife and kids ate the crust

of their bread probably because I had grown up believing t͟
the most nutritious part of the bread, and my wife was in ͟͟
of trimming the crust from her toast. By then, it was something I
said without even thinking about it, and my wife usually just smiled
in response. (And yes, that's right, husbands—she usually didn't eat
her crust.)

After breakfast, my Jeep driver grabbed my bags and went down
to the parking lot to wait for me. I gave my wife a kiss and headed
for the door when she stopped me and started to give me a little lecture before I left.

"Did you see what happened?" she asked.

"What do you mean?"

"That young man had taken the crust off his bread, too, and
when he heard you say, 'Eat your crust,' he began stuffing those
crusts into his face with both hands to make sure you weren't going
to say anything to him."

The reason I relate this story is because it says something about
the influence that compassionate leadership can exert. I don't think
this young soldier was afraid of getting reprimanded for not eating
his crust; I just believe he didn't want to disappoint the officer who
had shown him such consideration, abiding by that principle of
compassion, by offering him breakfast before a long trip. (If by
chance he reads this book, he'll know exactly who I'm talking about.)

So to me, living means giving, and I believe there is a reason the
two words are so similar. They are bound together, each dependent
on the other. Life is truly meaningful only so long as we are in some
way serving others. Leadership does not entitle one to abdicate the
responsibility of serving and giving. In fact, leadership is all about
giving, and to give wisely and effectively you've got to have that
innately human characteristic, that central principle of leadership:
compassion. That's why compassion is such a vital component of the
leadership formula.

Here's another story that will help you see how this works. When I was a brigade commander at Fort Knox, I was responsible for one of the first training brigades organized for the all-volunteer army. We were encountering a lot of things that our modern army had never experienced before. To their credit, the army's senior leaders during that time understood that there would be some big differences between volunteers and draftees, and our basic training cycle had to be adjusted to reflect those differences.

Basic training—a new recruit's first six weeks in the service—was something that had been studied very carefully, and adjustments to the training schedule, while necessary, placed new demands on the drill sergeants. These are the men (now joined by their female counterparts) who oversee the new recruits' training during this initial period, and they are vitally important to this introductory phase of the new recruits' experience. They're the ones on site with these young men and women, full time, day and night.

Drill sergeants fulfill one of the most demanding and responsible roles in the entire army. They seldom have a moment with their families except to change uniforms, enjoy a brief meal, and hustle back to the training cycle. With this life, the break between training cycles was a critical time to critique, rest, and recuperate as well as being extremely helpful for the morale of the drill sergeants and their families. Without this break, they could eventually become resentful and exhausted, creating the equally dangerous possibility that their emotions would be projected onto the new recruits. That, of course, would be a disastrous outcome since basic training was difficult enough for everyone involved. So the drill sergeants would endure a six-week training cycle, take some time off to be with their families, and then return for another cycle, hopefully with their batteries recharged and their humor intact.

Coincident with my arrival as the new brigade commander, the unit was enlarged by the merger of two smaller brigades into one large brigade. And the first of the new basic-training cycles was scheduled to start shortly after I assumed command.

As will happen in any large bureaucracy like the army, the schedule was put together at higher headquarters, and by unfortunate timing, it dictated that the new cycle for recruits would begin on the second of July, which was a Friday. This meant that the entire Fourth of July holiday weekend—and beyond—would have to be devoted to bringing in the new recruits, assigning them to barracks, and going through the early phases of basic-training orientation. These first few days of basic training are especially demanding, requiring almost full-time, twenty-four-hour-a-day dedication from the drill sergeants. It is mentally and physically exhausting and even more so with the new demands required to adapt to the all-volunteer army. The drill sergeants had been extensively trained and prepared for this experience, but in many ways, this first cycle of basic training would be the most rigorous and challenging they had ever experienced.

Now this was their job, obviously, and they were expected to embrace it with dignity, enthusiasm, and professionalism. They were, after all, the front-line leaders for the training of the army's new recruits. But I felt that some accommodation was warranted under the circumstances, so I approached the commanding general (I was a colonel at the time) and suggested that we consider delaying by just a few days the start of the next cycle of basic training.

"Why?" he asked.

"Sir, I just think if we let the men have their holiday weekend, we'll be better prepared to start the new cycle. We have to do a lot of preparation anyway; we can get all that done before the weekend."

After some discussion back and forth, we both decided that this was a good idea. It just didn't make sense to have all the drill sergeants there on July Fourth weekend . . . not when it was within our power to make a reasonable adjustment to the schedule. So the

CG did what he had to do to make the higher headquarters see it the way we did. For both of us, this was a compassionate act of leadership. And an aspiring leader would clearly understand why it was important for me (and for the commanding general) to make that decision—for the good of the men and women under my command.

Being compassionate does not imply softness; in no way should compassion be confused with weakness. I wasn't trying to make things easy for my drill sergeants. More than most soldiers, these men understood the importance of rigorous and challenging training. If my gesture had been interpreted as being just for my own benefit or if it had appeared that I was only trying to buy their friendship, they would instantly have lost respect for me.

When you're in training, it's important that there be some tough times and sacrifices because that's what's going to happen when the real fighting begins. But I made an educated assessment of the situation and came to the conclusion that the lives of the drill sergeants were hard enough and they deserved a couple days of rest with their families over this holiday weekend before embarking on a new training cycle.

Simply by making that kind of judgment as a new commander, I was able to set a tone that was very helpful in opening up the lines of communication within my subordinates and fostering a sense of trust among them. I knew intuitively that the drill sergeants would say to themselves, and to each other, "You know what? The old man is thinking about us." When you can transmit that kind of compassion—I care about you; I'm not trying to pamper you, but I care about you, and I think about those little things that help you and your family—it's a great benefit, particularly when you find yourself just starting off in a new position of leadership.

I know some may think it better to demonstrate how tough you can be by keeping to the schedule and showing up yourself day and night during those first few days. I would argue the reverse since conventional wisdom says that leaders are tough; they wouldn't have made it to command if they weren't. But taking advantage of an opportunity to exercise the other side of your leadership shows that you are not so rigid that others can't approach you or trust you. It shows that you're comfortable in your own skin. You are adaptable . . . confident . . . compassionate.

It's interesting, too, that the simplest acts of compassion can have such a profound impact on people. I was having dinner with my wife at the Thayer Hotel at West Point a few short years ago, when a well-groomed gentleman in his late forties or early fifties walked over to our table. It was early in the summer, right before the new plebe class was scheduled to enter its summer training, the infamous Beast Barracks. This gentleman was accompanied by his son, a recent high school graduate who had won appointment to the Academy and would soon be enrolling. As he shook my hand, the man explained that he had spotted me from across the dining room, had recognized me, and wanted to say hello and introduce me to his son.

Although he was a very pleasant and polite man, the introduction was a bit awkward because I could not recall ever having met him before. He went on to explain that he had served in the army during the Vietnam War. One day while on combat patrol in the Central Highlands, he was sitting on the side of a road, waiting for his platoon leader to return when I drove up in my Jeep.

"You were a battalion commander," he said. "And although I wasn't in your battalion, some of the soldiers in my platoon knew about you."

I nodded politely, hoping that what they knew about me was positive, but not sure where the story was headed.

"You stopped and walked over, and all the GIs stood up," the man continued. He paused and smiled. "And you said to me, 'Son, put your helmet on.'"

Ah, yes . . . the helmet. That was just one of the little articles of faith that every soldier in combat was wise to adopt. In Vietnam and Cambodia, you wore your helmet at all times because you never knew when the proverbial fat was going to hit the fire. Out in the boonies, there was always the risk of a sniper attack or a mortar round coming in. Something is always not far from happening in places like that, and in that war as in all wars, a helmet was an important piece of protection, albeit an uncomfortable one after long hours in the hot sun.

Despite all that, time and time again a soldier—especially a young soldier—seeking relief from the heat and humidity, would absentmindedly remove his helmet and not put it back on. To me, it was the simplest and most sensible thing in the world to remind these soldiers that they were taking an unnecessary risk if they remained uncovered for any length of time. I'm sure that sometimes they thought I was being overly cautious or fussy. After a few weeks (or even a few days) in country, however, they usually understood the situation and kept their helmets on. But we are all immortal at eighteen or nineteen, and I'm sure way back then this gentleman was no exception.

And here he was again, standing in front of me some three decades later, with his son about to enter West Point and become a leader of soldiers. He understood things in a different way, and I guess he was trying to thank me, for the tone of his voice, in repeating what I had said to him on that road in Vietnam, was that of a father gently speaking to a son . . . not a commander giving an order to a subordinate.

As you can well imagine, this little incident had a lasting impact on me, for it reinforced what I've always felt about leadership: people respond to a human touch, and compassion is rewarded with loyalty. When the gentleman and his son left, my wife smiled and said, "That's you exactly!"

"Really?"

"Absolutely. I can hear you saying those words; you always call all those young men 'son' because that's how you treat people. You have a lot of compassion in the way you treat them, and it really helps them relate to you. It makes you seem approachable."

I believe all of those things are true, just as I believe that a compassionate approach to leadership is the only one that makes sense.

10

VISION

If you don't know where you're going, you're liable to end up someplace else.

—DAVE CAMPBELL,
CENTER FOR CREATIVE LEADERSHIP

Great leaders often are described as *visionary,* but what does that mean?

In truth, there is more to vision than meets the eye. Some think of it in terms of being able to see far in advance the obstacles that must be cleared in order to complete a journey. And that's a true and accurate definition. But that's not all it is. Vision is also about reaching out to others and doing what has to be done. Visionaries not only anticipate problems and challenges; they immediately begin formulating ways to solve the problems—even if that means asking for help. Vision is an awareness of what must be done, as opposed to possessing some particular skill or intellect or clairvoyance that others do not possess. Cadets at West Point learn from the beginning that they must always look ahead to what's coming down the road, so vision becomes one of the principles of the leadership they learn.

Vision has another element that leaders must recognize and act upon. A leader by necessity looks to the future, and somewhere down the road must recognize there will come a time when ceding responsibility to new leadership is the right thing to do. At the Military Academy, each year brings new leaders to the fore as classes graduate and leave their positions of responsibility to the next in line. In a very real way, cadets begin preparing to exercise this element of vision as they rise from plebes to become graduates.

Vision is an awareness of what must be done, as opposed to possessing some particular skill or intellect or clairvoyance that others do not possess.

In the army, a similar transition takes place every few years as new assignments and promotions bring new leadership in place of the old, new ideas emerge to become reality, and leaders plan to turn over their current responsibilities to the next leadership team. To my mind, being educated and trained for leadership, then actually assuming and, finally, ceding the responsibilities of leadership in the structure of the army are the best preparation for life that a young person can ever find.

I have noted on several occasions in this book that I built my career on a foundation of focus and hard work; I concentrated on the task at hand and tried to do it to the best of my ability, with little regard for what might come next. But please don't mistake focus for myopia. Not looking around the corner for the next job does not necessarily reflect a lack of vision. Good leaders always look ahead, although not with personal aggrandizement in mind. Their concerns are for the soldiers in their platoons, or the people who work in their business unit. If their subordinates have the proper tools at their disposal, and they are prepared for changes in the marketplace, then they will be more likely to do a good job. This naturally reflects well on everyone, including the leader.

There is a fairly simple question that any leader of an organization would be wise to keep in mind: What am I supposed to do? If I'm a manager or vice president in the private sector, do I go down and help my directors run their divisions? Is that an intelligent approach to the job? Probably not, because eventually something will come along that nobody anticipated, and we'll all be scrambling to figure out what to do because no one thought about this ahead of time. No, my job in that situation is to look out—to help my people get ready for something new and unexpected that's coming down the pike; to try to eliminate as many of the unanticipated problems as we can.

Vision is then really central to that thought—that leaders look out; they oversee an organization that has a specific mission, and within the structure of that organization are subordinates who are charged to look inward. The army has an advantage: it's already set up that way. You come to the position as a commissioned officer, with noncommissioned officers who are very familiar with how the organization works. They already know all their troops, and their job is to look in while you, the newly commissioned officer, look out. Your job is to see the bigger picture. Admittedly, some of the noncommissioned officers may also be relatively new; they're young and learning the ropes and so forth. Nevertheless, that's their job: to communicate with the commissioned officer, to say, in effect, "Sir, this is our mission. Here's what we have to do to get the troops trained, here's the equipment we need, and this is how long it's going to take." The commissioned officer then takes this information and works to create an atmosphere in which the noncommissioned officers can accomplish their goals. I can't say this too many times: commissioned officers look out; NCOs look in.

During all my years in the army, I would often hear people talking about their achievements, when what they were really talking about was time on the job.

Vision should never be mistaken for clairvoyance. It's much more simple and attainable than that. Vision is nothing more (or less) than the ability to see how parts work together. Like anything else, vision is a talent, and some leaders are more naturally adept at it than others. They're shrewd and smart, and they have a natural instinct for understanding how things and people work. This quality might give them a little bit of an advantage; they may have some indication in their own minds about what's going to happen next.

Remember, though, that experience is a great informer of vision. The more time you've logged on a job, the better you'll be at figuring out what's going to happen in the coming months or years, assuming, of course, that you've been paying attention. Simply by virtue of having been in a position of leadership for a period of time and having accrued knowledge about the way things work, you're more likely to anticipate curves in the road. If the curve never appears or goes the other way . . . well, then a self-assessment is in order: What happened? Why did you miscalculate or not see this coming?

The basic element in vision is to learn from your experience—from your mistakes and your accomplishments. During all my years in the army, I would often hear people talking about their achievements, when what they were really talking about was time on the job.

"I've got twenty years in battalions," they might say.

And I'd find myself wondering, *Well, does that mean you have twenty years of experience . . . or one year of experience twenty times?*

★ ★ ★

Nothing stunts growth more than surrounding yourself with *yes men* and believing everything they tell you.

Leadership experience informs your vision—as long as you are continually growing and learning. The reverse is also true. If you convince yourself that you have nothing more to learn simply because you've been in the same place, doing the same job for whatever number of years, it can actually inhibit your vision. Familiarity not only breeds contempt; it also can breed laziness and complacency. The lessons are ongoing, and growth never ends. You can't expect to have all the answers when you become a leader for the first time, can you? Well, I have news for you: when you retire forty years later, you still won't have all the answers. Along the way you'll be wise to ask a lot of questions and to surround yourself with people you can trust to tell it to you like it is. Nothing stunts growth more than surrounding yourself with *yes men* and believing everything they tell you. That's a crucial component of the leadership principle known as vision: looking ahead and preparing for the next challenge.

To do this, you'll need help. Training for leadership is preparing for life, and among all the other preparations to be made, seeking assistance has to be one of them. Good leaders understand that they are always in the business of training new leaders, and the people they train have to be trustworthy and loyal, for there will be times when their leaders must turn to them for help. Why? Because vision involves acknowledging one's weaknesses; none of us is infallible. Here is where vision overlaps with confidence because realizing a vision involves not only looking ahead but also doing whatever is necessary to make the vision a reality. Even if it means asking for help.

LEADING FOR TODAY, LOOKING TO TOMORROW

Vision represents an amalgamation of skills—an ability to be creative when you're melding what's happening right now, in the present, with what may (or may not) be happening tomorrow. In so many ways, vision is the most important and challenging principle of leadership, for it demands that a leader continue to create an environment in which subordinates can function at a high level, performing all of the tasks required of an organization, while simultaneously preparing for the changes that will inevitably occur.

In the business world, the sales staff continues hard at work, even as the research and development department strives to create new products that will ultimately replace (or at least supplement) those currently on the market. They are two different branches of the same sturdy tree, and it is the leader with vision who nurtures both with equal diligence. Leaders cannot just close their minds to the problems of the future simply because the burden of surviving seems to take all their energies every day.

Vision is the most important and challenging principle of leadership, for it demands that a leader continue to create an environment in which subordinates can function at a high level, performing all of the tasks required of an organization, while simultaneously preparing for the changes that will inevitably occur.

Nor can they fall victim to the trap of believing that change isn't necessary since the soldiers are performing and the mission is going well, or business is good and people are buying their products. We've all heard the saying, "If it ain't broke, don't fix it!" Well, guess what? Eventually, even if *it* doesn't break, something else is going to happen that renders it obsolete or, even worse, a detriment to the organization. Don't wait for that day to come. The problems of tomorrow eventually become the problems of today—that's inevitable. Theoretically, when that day comes, if you are a commissioned officer in the army, you will have already provided the resources to your subordinates so they can look in and get the job done in the best way they can. That same approach applies to the business world as well.

As with all of these principles, vision is at once a skill (something that can be learned and refined) and a talent. You don't have to be a genius to develop vision and to apply it to your everyday life as a leader. Some people seem to possess an innate ability to see the big picture better than others. They are more adept at juggling current responsibilities while anticipating what may be coming next. I saw this on a regular basis when I was a cadet at West Point and at every assignment throughout my career. When I became the commandant, it was at once interesting and tremendously rewarding to see how proximity to the young men and women in the Corps of Cadets, combined with my own life experience, afforded me the opportunity to make an educated guess as to which cadets seemed to have a gift for vision.

My hunches were sometimes wrong, but usually I could see something in a young man or woman—a spark not instantly recognizable in others—that led me to believe this was someone special. I mentioned in the previous chapter the story of a cadet who was suspended during my tenure as commandant. He was an extremely likable, charismatic, and talented young man who possessed many of the traits necessary to be a successful officer in the army—and, indeed, to be successful in just about any walk of life. But he was a spirited, energetic, and largely undisciplined young man as well. He had a mischievous streak in him, no question about it. But the more I talked with this young man and the more I talked with others who knew him, the more I became convinced that he had enormous potential. So I faced a dilemma: Do I permanently dismiss a gifted cadet . . . or tolerate his immaturity and hope that he would change?

This young man's behavior was disruptive, particularly to his own development—and if you let something like that go on unchecked, then what sort of message are you sending to the miscreant (and to others in his sphere of influence)? The best compromise, in my opinion, was to hand out a one-year suspension, then permit him to apply for reinstatement. Fortunately, this particular cadet took the lesson to heart and returned to West Point with a renewed sense of purpose, as well as a commitment to behaving in an appropriate manner. In simple terms, he found a way to focus his vast supply of energy, and both he and the army benefited in the long run. This was a man who became an exemplary military officer and a highly accomplished businessman. He had vision. A bit blurry, perhaps, in the beginning, but he had it nonetheless.

And I should add that I used my vision as well. It is indeed a great reward when vision is confirmed by experience. Let's not overlook the role that faith also played in my decision. The mosaic that displays the principles of leadership is indeed interwoven and tightly bound.

PROMOTED ON THE FAST TRACK

Just like the army, the system at West Point is designed not only to develop and train leaders but also, as with any successful leadership model, to target and promote those who appear to have the greatest potential. Cadets who are candidates for advancement—from the highest positions in their chain of command on down—are selected based on the evaluations and recommendations of tactical officers, tac NCOs, instructors, coaches, and others who see them in action each day. It's a thoughtful, careful process replete with interviews and tests, but it's not an infallible system.

I can think of examples during my own time as a cadet—classmates who graduated with lots of stripes and could thus be considered early candidates for accelerated promotion. The first time in my career that the army adopted an accelerated promotion system was in the early sixties, when promising officers who were "below the zone" (that is, junior to the regular-year groups of officers to be considered for promotion) were selected for promotion ahead of their peers. Basically, it worked like this: if two thousand officers were to be selected for promotion based on length of service (the "zone" for consideration) and credible performance, a small percentage of those being promoted would come from a group that was deemed below the zone.

Typically, the percentage of below-the-zone promotions was very small—less than 5 percent of the total number selected—and to appear on that list was considered quite an accomplishment. I had a classmate on that list the first time we reached below-the-zone status when we were considered for promotion from captain to major. He was—at a very young age—a superstar. But you know what? Several years later when we were first considered for regular promotion from major to lieutenant colonel, he was passed over for regular promotion with his peers! And that was that. This man, a very capable and hardworking officer, eventually was promoted, but he retired as a lieutenant colonel. He wasn't a failure—he had just sort of reached a plateau that was his limit.

I find that story to be somewhat instructive. There are people in all walks of life who, early on, zoom out there in front of the pack, and then they get reeled back in when life intrudes. Disciplinary problems, health issues, family responsibilities—these things can all truncate a career. It's possible at West Point to look at the youngest folks and make some fairly reasonable assessments about leadership potential. In fact, it would be irresponsible *not* to do that. And we do indeed select young men and women to be officers while they're still cadets—officers in the sense that they are selected to be cadet leaders, to set an example for the rest of the Corps of Cadets. That's a terrific experience; it's a leadership opportunity that carries real responsibility, and as such it places a significant demand on the cadet, compelling him to lead and to think rather than to follow. He must ask himself each day, *What am I supposed to do? What are the principles I'm exercising? How do I apply them?*

Exposure to great leaders, and to people of vision, is also a building block of the West Point experience. I'll give you a couple of examples. As a football player, I actually met General Douglas MacArthur. This was in the early fifties, and he was by then retired from the army. But he and the coach, Colonel Earl "Red" Blaik, had been close ever since Blaik was the captain of the football team during MacArthur's tenure as superintendent at West Point in the twenties.

So in my time as a cadet, General MacArthur would come to West Point on occasion, usually during spring practice, and afterward he would stop by the locker room to greet the players. It was, to say the least, an interesting experience for me as a young cadet. Here was a gentleman whom we all knew as a great and revered leader. The first thing I noticed was that he was not as large as he appeared in photos, but he was very well turned out in a Chesterfield coat and an immaculate gray homburg.

With a commanding presence, even at his advancing age, General MacArthur surprised us by knowing every player's name. I found that hugely impressive. After all, there was nothing to identify us—no names on the jerseys or lockers. Just uniform numbers. But there was General Douglas MacArthur, strolling through the locker room, shaking hands, addressing player after player by name: "Franklin, how are you today?"

That is the sort of thing that sticks with you.

Yet of even greater importance to me, personally, was an interaction with Coach Blaik on the day I graduated from the Academy (as great to me at the time as shaking hands with President Eisenhower, who distributed diplomas that day): "Nice going,

Franklin," he said when I took my diploma from him. In all the time I'd known Colonel Blaik, who was himself a great icon to us and to college football, I'd never heard him address a player by anything other than his surname. I was always Franklin to him, as in, "Franklin, get back in the game!" After graduation, however, as I walked past the gymnasium, diploma in hand, I heard a familiar voice calling me from above.

"Franklin, wait right there!"

I looked up. There was Colonel Blaik, looking down at me from his office window. A few moments later we were standing on the sidewalk face-to-face, and Colonel Blaik extended his hand. With a broad and disarming smile, unlike anything I'd seen as a football player, he said, "Joseph, my lad, send us some more like you."

I wasn't sure Coach Blaik even knew my first name. I was not a star by any measure, and even though I played for him for three years, I had never heard him use it. But that was okay by me, for Red Blaik, with all that he had achieved and the image he projected, was one of those men you may meet only once or twice in a lifetime. They live above the clouds. The fact that here was someone like him, who would say words like that to someone like me . . . well, what an inspiration! Why did he do that? Perhaps it was his own vision, having seen my perseverance and glimmers of leadership on the field, but Colonel Blaik did that day what great leaders do: by calling on his vision, he inspired his subordinate to do his best when he went on to his army career.

To this day, I carry the memory of that exchange, and I have always looked for opportunities to touch someone else in a similar manner. Not that I consider my accomplishments to be comparable to those of Colonel Blaik, but his gracious gesture constantly reminds me of the importance of reaching out to those you might influence, especially youngsters. It can be something as simple as inquiring about a family member or complimenting a subordinate on a job well done.

Use your vision; you can figure out how to do this.

★ ★ ★

Vision, which goes hand-in-hand with adaptability, is a key principle of leadership because everything is subject to change.

Colonel Blaik understood that, which is why he was such a great and visionary leader. Years later, when I became the commandant, he wrote me a letter of congratulations. "Dear Joe," it began. "That you are to be the commandant is a source of great pride for me, and a signal that football players are long on leadership." Colonel Blaik was living out his final years in Colorado Springs, so I called him up and arranged to interview him for an in-house project about leadership and athletics.

Colonel Blaik's letter is now framed and occupies a prominent place in my home. It is a constant reminder to me of how much influence a leader can have upon others. The interview I conducted with Coach Blaik was a lively dialogue about football, the plebe system at West Point, and the value of athletics in an educational and military setting. I still have a copy on DVD, and I have heard that it's shown to the football team every year. Colonel Blaik was a true visionary—I can see that now when I watch the DVD.

Others, of course, saw Earl Blaik's potential at a much younger age. When he was still a cadet, he was selected by the superintendent, General MacArthur, to be the senior cadet on an officer-cadet committee charged to completely revise the plebe system. He accomplished that task, but he also had the wisdom and the foresight to understand that the overhaul would not be permanent, that all things are cyclical, and that the plebe system would need constant oversight and updating on a regular basis. Colonel Blaik knew that something as vital and volatile as the plebe system at West Point would never be chiseled in stone. Improvement and modernization would always be needed to keep the system current with the demands of the modern military profession. He was, in truth, a leader of great vision.

If you don't know where you're going, it's hard to get there, isn't it? And like it or not, you're probably going to wind up someplace else. In the armed forces, for example, we are charged with preparing to meet not only the threats facing our country today but also potential threats that may be faced in the future. Vision, which goes hand-in-hand with adaptability, is a key principle of leadership because everything is subject to change. To deny change, or to ignore its inevitability, is to court failure.

Consider this: one of the great businesses of the nineteenth century was the manufacturing of bridles, harnesses, and saddles for horses. It was an enormous and lucrative industry—until the internal combustion engine came along shortly after the turn of the century, and suddenly people were no longer utilizing large numbers of horses for work and transportation. Did anyone in the harness business see this coming? And what did they do to adapt to the inevitable impacts on their industry? Vision (which fuels adaptability) is crucial to the long-term health of any business venture.

Let me return to the case of Frequency Electronics. When I joined the company in 1992, we had a subsidiary in California that had developed a small, very capable timing system, the foundation of which was a crystal stabilized by an atomic process utilizing the element rubidium. Some of our engineers—the older, senior men—were very impressed with the technology and efficiency of this product, and I can vividly remember them saying,

"You know, this rubidium oscillator is really a little jewel." When we sold that portion of the company, that little jewel was very small in terms of the amount of business it would generate. Yet we kept it in our inventory and brought it back to New York because our engineers were shrewd enough and smart enough to recognize the product's future potential. Ten years later, that little jewel had become almost half of Frequency's business, and thanks to its success, the company's total business had almost tripled in volume!

That's the value of vision.

VISION FUELS ADAPTABILITY

Similarly, in the military, if you are a young officer looking ahead to your growth as a leader, you can't lose sight of the fact that you exist in a world where vision that fuels adaptability is a prerequisite. You have orders that must be carried out, but you also have to recognize that every situation is going to require you to adapt to changing circumstances. You have to be looking ahead at what might be coming, using your vision to guide your next moves. A sound strategy always is to think about and prepare alternatives, to ensure that even if things turn out differently than you anticipated, you'll be ready to react in an appropriate and effective manner. A certain portion of each workday should be devoted to thinking about and planning for the future; in that way, you'll be able to adapt and move forward, regardless of the obstacles that will inevitably lumber into your path.

When I first joined the military, over a half century ago, the helicopter was a very small part of our arsenal. They were clumsy, piston-driven vehicles limited in usefulness for combat, and because early versions were fragile and sometimes unpredictable in performance, they were somewhat dangerous. We used them mostly for observation, and even in that regard their limitations precluded widespread implementation.

But as those capabilities increased, in terms of transport, communication, and combat, the helicopter became an indispensable piece of military equipment, one that really altered the face of the military. Did I anticipate such a revolutionary change? No, it was never really part of my duties until I was a battalion commander in Vietnam. Then I came face-to-face with the combat capabilities that others had foreseen, and I was extremely thankful for it. Others of my contemporaries had the vision to see these capabilities and had joined the ranks of helo pilots, eventually rising high up in the army's leadership as a result. They had vision.

Some people cling to the past, for better or worse. I clearly remember walking by Hubb's Harness Shop in Oakland, Maryland, the morning after the atomic bomb was dropped on Hiroshima in August 1945. I was twelve years old at the time, and uncertain of the significance of this event, but I can still recall seeing two old gentlemen in bib overalls sitting on a bench outside the shop, leaning forward on their canes, talking to each other as if reminiscing about other days gone by.

The first gentleman spoke: "I still say the worst thing that ever happened in warfare was Sherman's march across Georgia!"

The other nodded in agreement.

"They even burned the shoes of the little children so they wouldn't have anything to put on their feet. Nothing could be worse than that."

I can remember that conversation as vividly as I can recall what I had for breakfast this morning. Even as a raw adolescent from rural Appalachian Maryland, I understood that I was listening to two men who believed with all their hearts that things worked a certain way. These were men unlikely to accept the notion of change or the concept of adaptability. At their stage in life, these were not men of vision. They were, I'm quite sure, good men, strong and thoughtful in their own way, and they'd doubtless been told all about Sherman's march and his scorched-earth approach to war. To them, it was inconceivable that anything could surpass in brutality or effectiveness this legendary Civil War onslaught. The atomic bomb, of course, changed everything and set a new and horrific standard for strategic warfare. Nothing else compared; nothing else came close.

Vision involves an awareness of the world around you, an acute sense that everything can and will change. One thing is certain: a leader without vision is lost. And a leader who lacks vision and the ability to adapt is . . . well . . . in the end, really not a leader at all. Leaders not only understand this and prepare for it but also work to transmit to those around them—not just subordinates but contemporaries and superiors as well—the importance of preparing for the future, for the day will come when the world will be a very different place. You really don't want to wake up and find that you were asleep at the wheel when that happens.

Listen to those around you. Keep your eyes and ears open. Learn from those above you, as well as those below you. In the army, senior officers are very attentive to what junior officers have to say, and not merely to be courteous. It's a matter of practicality. Things change rapidly, and what the junior officers have learned in their brief lifetimes is far more than what we who are now old soldiers learned in our own equivalent lifetimes. That's just a simple, indisputable fact. Because of the way the world is today, because of what the media and other commentators can transmit through the myriad channels of communications, and because of the increasing demands placed on youngsters in our educational system, junior officers in the army today are much more knowledgeable than were their counterparts of only a few decades past.

> **The day will come when the world will be a very different place. You really don't want to wake up and find that you were asleep at the wheel when that happens.**

Vision, then, involves not only developing leadership skills in subordinates but also drawing on the experiences of the subordinates themselves. Try to think of leadership as a circle rather than a pyramid, and you'll get the picture. You are at the center, rather than the top. Information flows from the center to the perimeter and back again. It flows in all directions at once. Leaders have to absorb as much information as possible, from as many sources as possible, and make decisions based on instinct, intelligence, heart, and guts. They have to understand that even though they are at the center of the circle, they are not the center of the universe. Their job is important, but temporary. They are caretakers, responsible for their mission and all that happens to their subordinates. Then, ultimately, they must pass that responsibility on to the next caretakers.

But then, you probably already knew that because you have vision.

You are a leader.

Afterword

LOOKING AHEAD

No generalization is worth a damn, including this one.
—OLIVER WENDELL HOLMES

If this book accomplishes only one thing, I hope it will be to disabuse the reader of any notion that leadership is as easy as figuring out where the crowd is going and running around to get in front of it. Leadership is a hard, often lonely pursuit, but it is there for those willing to work for it.

I have also quietly derided the idea that leaders should hand down their knowledge from some elevated oracle, and I hope I have avoided that trap in writing this book. Thus, I urge all who read these words to take them as a colloquium and not a sermon.

Nothing that I've written here is rocket science. Like so much of leadership, common sense and accumulated wisdom will prove to be your greatest allies as responsibilities increase and leadership responsibilities grow. For those of you just stepping into the complex, challenging, and enormously rewarding world of leadership, it would help to have a detailed road map for success. But there is no such thing. What I am trying to provide here is some practical advice that you can use as you acquire the experience to give our nation the good, effective leadership we will need to carry us through the turbulent times ahead. They will, without doubt, be the times that try men's souls.

There are, as I have noted, many others with more experience than I who can add a great deal to this colloquium, and I urge them to add their thoughts to this library of leadership know-how. I have written down my own thoughts as one man's contribution with hopes that others will be moved to do the same. Our fledgling leaders deserve no less than we "old soldiers" can offer. The more I see and learn of the young men and women in today's army, the more convinced I become that they are, in truth, America's next greatest generation. They are our future leaders, and they carry the hopes of the free world in their rucksacks. Go Army! Go USA!

If we don't learn from history, we are doomed to repeat it.
—With a salute to the wisdom of Socrates

ABOUT THE AUTHOR

MAJOR GENERAL JOSEPH P. FRANKLIN, U.S. Army (Retired), was born in 1933 in Cumberland, Maryland. In 1951, Franklin won a competitive appointment to the U.S. Military Academy and graduated in 1955 with a commission in the U.S. Army Corps of Engineers.

After preliminary military schooling, which included Parachute and Ranger qualification, Franklin was assigned to Karlsruhe, Germany, and served with combat engineer units until 1959. He was then sent to MIT to earn master's degrees in civil engineering and nuclear engineering, and in 1961 was assigned to the Army Nuclear Power Program, headquartered at Fort Belvoir, Virginia, where he worked as project manager to install a nuclear power plant on board a converted Liberty ship. In 1963, he was assigned to the command of Camp Century, a nuclear-powered research outpost on the Greenland ice cap. He directed the shutdown and disassembly of the nuclear power plant, shipping the entire facility back to the U.S. in 1964.

Selected for instructor duty at West Point in 1965, Franklin taught West Point's first nuclear engineering course and coached the football and ski teams during his three years as a professor. After a year's further study at the Naval War College, he shipped out to Vietnam to command a combat engineer battalion in the Central Highlands, ending his tour after participating in the 1970 invasion of Cambodia. The decade of the seventies was taken up with Pentagon duty, including a tour as executive assistant to the chairman of the Joint Chiefs of Staff, plus a brigade command at Fort Knox, Kentucky, and another year of study at the Army War College.

Promoted to brigadier general in 1979, Franklin was selected to be commandant of cadets at West Point where he served until 1982. A tour of duty as assistant commander of the Twenty-fifth Infantry Division in Hawaii was followed by promotion to major general and assignment in 1983 as chief of the Joint U.S. Military Group and senior U.S. defense representative in Spain.

Franklin chose to retire in 1987 and remained in Spain, founding Franklin, S.A., a Spanish business consultancy located in Madrid, specializing in investments and joint ventures. He was elected to the board of directors of several Spanish and American companies, one of which was Frequency Electronics at Mitchel Field, New York. He returned to the U.S. in 1993, when he was elected chairman of the board and chief executive officer of Frequency Electronics. He continues to serve as chairman of the board today, leaving the CEO position in 1999.

In 1996, Franklin became chairman of the board of advisors of the West Point Project, LLC—a group of private investors joined together to promote the U.S. Military Academy in cooperation with its Association of Graduates during West Point's bicentennial year. His work included the publication in 2002 of the bicentennial book: *West Point: Two Centuries of Honor and Tradition.* He also served as vice chairman of the board of trustees of the Association of Graduates.

In 2007, Franklin received West Point's Distinguished Graduate award, noting his outstanding career and fine example of the Academy's *Duty, Honor, Country* motto. He is presently on the board of directors of RKO Pictures, Inc., and is a former trustee of the McDonogh School in Baltimore, Maryland. He is married to Constance Marie Smith, also from Cumberland, Maryland. They have four sons and eight grandchildren.